Scott & Marty
my friends, always live
a creative life ♥

Hugs,
Lisa m Pace

delight
IN THE
seasons

Crafting a Year of
Memorable Holidays
and Celebrations

Lisa M. Pace

NORTH LIGHT BOOKS
CINCINNATI, OHIO

joyful

happy birthday

Contents

Introduction

Each season of the year is filled not only with holidays, but also with many special occasions and memorable events. I hope, as you flip through this book, you will find loads of inspiration for all that is celebrated during the seasons. In each chapter, you will find cards, tags, layouts and decorative items that can be given as gifts or used to commemorate occasions from the everyday to the extraordinary.

In Chapter One, you'll find projects for a holiday I love—Christmas. But Christmas isn't the only winter holiday; we'll also create projects for Valentine's Day as well as general winter cheer. I celebrate some of my spring memories in Chapter Two, including Easter, Mother's Day, Father's Day and more. I hope these techniques and projects will help you enjoy and remember your own springtime holidays and special occasions! Next comes summer, a time filled with celebration. In addition to plain old summer fun, Chapter Three features projects for birthdays, weddings, anniversaries and summer travel. Finally, we'll explore the holidays and special occasions of autumn, including Halloween, another favorite of mine. Along with Halloween, Chapter Four has projects and techniques for Grandparents Day, Thanksgiving and more.

Finally, I'll show you how to take the techniques in each chapter and use them to celebrate all of the seasons. Look through More Seasonal Delights, starting on page 114, to see how the techniques in this book can be transformed to suit more than one season.

All of the projects you'll see in these pages have a slight vintage feel, as I have incorporated my signature embellishments, such as vintage buttons, glass glitter, trims and pearls. If you like this look, you can replicate it yourself, or give each technique and project your own spin. With the many wonderful art and craft supplies available today, it's easy to put your own stamp on your projects. My hope is that while you browse through this book, you will find ways to create and accent projects that celebrate all the wonderful special occasions and memorable moments that are sprinkled throughout the seasons. Maybe you'll even be inspired to start a few creative traditions for your family. And remember: While you're busy creating and celebrating, always take delight in the seasons.

My Life in the Seasons

Growing up, I always looked forward to each season. In southeast Texas, we mainly had two seasons: winter and summer. As winter approached, the one thing I had in mind was the two-week Christmas break we had from school every year. I can remember getting so excited as Christmas got closer because that meant extra arts and crafts in school. I loved making paper and clay ornaments to bring home for our tree and using spray paint and glitter to turn a thick magazine into a tabletop tree decoration. My mom and I made things together at home to celebrate Christmas. Over the years, we've made raffia baskets, dough ornaments and cloth ornaments, as well as paper ornaments and numerous treats. Obviously, the love of crafting that I felt then is here to stay!

As much as winter makes me think of holidays, spring holds its own special occasions. I looked forward to watching the spring flowers bloom, but as fast as spring came, it left again as the hot Texas summer started. My family would take advantage of what little spring we had, though! One of my favorite times in spring was Easter. As spring approached, my mom and I looked forward to making bird nest cupcakes for Easter. When we made our cupcakes, I loved adding the green food coloring and shredded coconut to the icing to make the grass. Once my sister was old enough, she joined in the fun and she loved putting the jelly bean eggs on top of the shredded coconut topping. Deciding which colors to put on each cupcake was the hardest part. Another tradition in my house was that my mom and dad would always hide Easter eggs for us kids to find. Let me just say, some were pretty challenging to find. We found one egg behind a basket several years after it had been hidden. We still cannot understand why that thing did not smell! I guess it had been sitting there all that time waiting to be found.

Our short spring would quickly turn into summer and then my brother and I would run around the block barefoot and fancy-free all day long with not one care in the world. One summer, we created our own Slip 'n Slide using a water hose and a piece of plastic that covered the entire front yard. We and all the neighborhood kids had an incredible day of slipping and sliding. However, when mom and dad came home from work and saw the lovely mud pit their front yard had become, my brother Richard and I headed right up to our rooms without even needing to be told. But I have to tell you, we had a blast, the yard did recover, and my mom and dad weren't too hard on us. We were just kids having fun on a hot summer day. Summer for my family was also marked by a two-week trip to visit my grandparents. It was fun seeing our grandparents, aunts, uncles and cousins. We would all have big picnics and visit the old homestead where my grandmother cooked on the wood-burning stove. Another summer tradition was that on July 4th we would attend a pool party and spend the day swimming and playing games, then in the evening we would either sit on our garage roof or go down to the warehouse my mom and dad owned and climb up onto the roof there to watch the fireworks. It was fun to be so high up because it seemed like you could reach out and touch the brilliant fireworks. It was always sad to see summer end because of all the fun we had.

Once autumn started to hit Texas, we were back in school, excited to attend football games and enjoy the state fair. In the autumn, my mom always enjoyed helping me and my siblings get our costumes ready for Halloween. We never purchased ours; we just dug around in mom and dad's closet and made our own. One year, Mom dressed up as Mother Goose and hosted a Halloween party for all of the kids in the neighborhood. It was so much fun, and it is one of my favorite holiday memories.

I've poured my love of the seasons into the techniques and projects you'll see on the following pages, and I hope they help you share your special memories, too!

chapter one

Winter

Winter is the season that holds some of my favorite holidays. I have many wonderful memories of creating ornaments and other seasonal decorations with my mom while sitting at the kitchen table during Christmastime. I eagerly waited for my dad to make his homemade eggnog (the kid-safe version, of course), and I loved nibbling on all the special treats Mom and I would make together. Every Valentine's Day, my dad brought my mom a box filled with the best chocolates and a bouquet of beautiful roses with a card written to "Nugget." My mom says he called her Nugget when they first started dating because he couldn't remember her name, Juanita. Dad denies this—I find it cute either way. I do know one thing: I really wish I had the heart-shaped candy boxes from all those years. They just don't make them like they used to!

In this chapter, I will show you how to create items for the holidays and special occasions found in winter. Turn to page 20 to create a simple reflector out of foil cupcake liners; these are similar to the ones my grandmother used to put on her tree lights each Christmas. On page 30, you will learn how to create a patina effect using acrylic paints and ink on chipboard pieces. These embellished chipboard pieces accent a Valentine's Day banner perfectly. I will also show you how to create a beautiful layout using multiple photos for a winter-themed vignette and a heartwarming layout using the scanned image of a love letter. The techniques shared in this chapter are sure to inspire your creativity while you're sitting warm and toasty in your craft room. You might even get to watch snowflakes drifting slowly to the ground outside your window as you re-create these projects. Being from Texas, where snow is not at all common, watching a snowfall is one of the things about winter I find magical and inspiring. Enjoy all the facets of winter as you peruse these projects.

Air-Dry Clay 3-D Embellishment

Using an air-dry clay is a great way to create unique lightweight 3-D embellishments. To cut the clay into shapes, I like to use cookie cutters. These are perfect since they come in a wide variety of shapes and sizes. To create different textures on my clay embellishments, I like to use crocheted doilies, burlap and other heavily textured fabrics or materials, such as embossing plates. Once dry, your embellishment can be painted, inked and, of course, glittered.

Supplies: patterned paper (3ndypapir.no); air-dry modeling clay (C-Thru Ruler Company); paint (Making Memories); doily (Wilton); ultra thick embossing enamel, glitter glue, ink, pearlescent pigment spray (Ranger); ink (Clearsnap); punch (Fiskars); chipboard wings (Maya Road); felt (CPE); other: crocheted doily, vintage buttons, vintage sheet music, seam binding

What You'll Need

air-dry modeling clay, nonstick craft sheet, rolling pin, cookie cutter, crocheted doily, acrylic paint, paintbrush, paper towel, Perfect Medium Pen, Ultra Thick Embossing Enamel (UTEE), heat tool, glitter glue

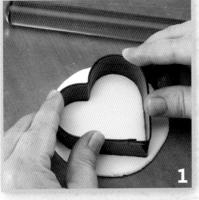

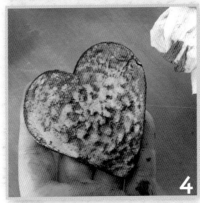

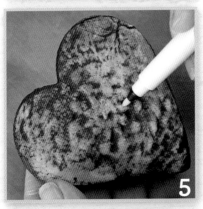

1 Form the air-dry modeling clay into a ball. Place the ball of clay onto a nonstick craft sheet and flatten it out using a rolling pin. Roll the clay until it is larger than the cookie cutter you are using. Press the cookie cutter into the clay. Remove the excess clay around the cut shape.

2 Place a crocheted doily onto the top of the clay piece; using the rolling pin, roll back and forth over the doily, applying a slight, even pressure. Gently remove the doily from the clay and let the clay air dry. If you do not have a crocheted doily, you can also use textured fabrics or even plastic embossing plates to create an embossed pattern.

3 Once the clay is dry, paint the entire piece with acrylic paint.

4 While the paint is still wet, wipe it off from all raised areas using a damp paper towel.

5 Mark the raised areas with a perfect medium pen. Mark only a small area so that the medium does not dry while you are working.

6 While the medium is wet, sprinkle white UTEE over the marked areas.

7 Tap off the excess UTEE and melt it using a heat tool. Repeat steps 5-7 over the surface of the entire heart.

8 Once the UTEE is completely cooled, accent the raised areas using glitter glue (I used Diamond and Icicle Stickles). Outline the outer edge of the piece using platinum glitter glue as well.

Altered Tart Tin

Tart tins are great items to use as the base of a project or to add to a project. They can usually be found in antique shops and thrift stores and cost very little. I like to use tart tins in two different sizes for my projects. In this trio, I used tins in the larger size, but mini tart tins are perfect for smaller projects. Here, I've altered three different tins to create an ornament, a magnet and a brooch. I've chosen to make my tins colorful, but if you want a tarnished look for your project, apply light brown alcohol ink to the tin's edges and creases with a cotton swab; this will add the perfect tint for an aged look.

Supplies: patterned paper (3ndypapir.no); tinsel (Bethany Lowe); ink (Clearsnap); chipboard foundations (Maya Road); glitter glue, alcohol ink (Ranger); sisal wreath, doily, holiday embellishments (Hobby Lobby); glitter (EK Success); pin back (Darice); rhinestones (Advantus); other: tart tin, seam binding, vintage accents, beads, baker's twine

What You'll Need

tart tin, alcohol ink, cotton swab, chipboard pieces, photo, craft knife, cutting mat, glue, sanding block, liquid adhesive, mini tinsel garland, scissors, foam squares, vintage embellishments, seam binding, beads, paper piercer, fabric adhesive

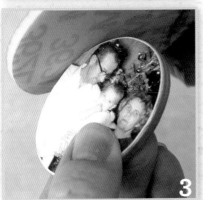

1 Apply alcohol ink to a cotton swab. Rub the alcohol ink over the entire tart tin. Your tin is now custom-colored for the project of your choice! To make the tart tin ornament featured on the previous page, follow the steps below.

2 Glue 2 oval chipboard pieces together and allow the glue to dry. Glue your photo to the chipboard pieces, centering it. Allow the glue to dry, then lay the photo facedown on a cutting mat and cut the photo around the chipboard pieces using a craft knife.

3 Sand the edges of the photo with a sanding block.

4 Apply liquid adhesive to the outer edge of the chipboard piece and attach the mini tinsel garland. Let the glue dry completely.

5 Adhere foam squares to the back of the chipboard, then place it inside the tart tin. Place the chipboard toward the top of the open space, leaving room at the bottom.

6 Apply liquid adhesive to the bottom portion of the tart tin and attach vintage embellishments there.

7 Cut an 18" (46cm) piece of seam binding and fold it in half. Thread 3 beads onto seam binding; use a thin paper piercer to push the seam binding through the hole in the bead if needed.

8 Lay the tart tin on top of the beaded seam binding. Space the beads so that 2 are at the top of the tart tin and 1 is at the bottom. Apply fabric adhesive to the back of the tart tin and adhere it to the seam binding.

Tissue Paper Trim

This cheerful card proclaims Valentine's Day wishes with lace, glitter and a pretty red-and-white tissue paper trim. With so many different decorative scissors available, you don't have to limit yourself to scallop scissors. You can use any kind of decorative-edge scissors to create a unique edging on your tissue paper trim. For a larger version of this trim, cut wider strips and add more strips to the stack before sewing and cutting.

Supplies: patterned paper, mini calendar (Jenni Bowlin); button (Making Memories); doily (Wilton); ink (Clearsnap); self-adhesive pearls (The Paper Studio); distress crackle paint, glitter glue (Ranger); satin pleat trim (Maya Road); leaves (Laura's Vintage Garden); other: tissue paper, baker's twine

What You'll Need

tissue paper (two colors), paper trimmer, sewing machine and thread, scallop scissors, straight scissors, ink

1 Cut 4 strips each of red tissue paper and white tissue paper. Each of the 8 strips should measure 1" × 12" (3cm × 30cm). Layer the strips of tissue paper, alternating the colors.

2 Using a sewing machine, sew with a straight stitch up the center of the stack.

3 Trim both 12" (30cm) edges of the stack using scallop scissors.

4 Cut between each scallop with straight scissors. Do not cut through the stitching. Repeat this step on each side of the sewn line.

5 Fold the tissue paper stack in half along the sewn line. Scrunch and ruffle the tissue paper to open up the fringe.

6 Lightly ink the tissue paper.

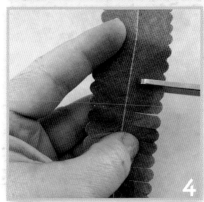

FEBRUARY

Paint and Ink Distressing

During the holiday season, it's easy to find small seasonal embellishments in any craft store. Items like these are easy to personalize for your friends and family. Some come already embellished in different themes, including those for girls, boys, moms, dads, aunts and uncles. Adding your own touch with paint and ink, like I've done here with this gift tag, is an easy way to add that "special something" to a gift.

Supplies: party favor tray (Wilton); paint (Making Memories); ink (Clearsnap); glitter glue (Ranger); chalkboard spray paint (Krylon); other: holly, candy canes, baker's twine

What You'll Need

party favor tray, chalkboard spray paint, acrylic paint (three colors), paintbrush, ink, sanding block, glitter glue, miniature candy canes, holly leaves, baker's twine, strong liquid adhesive, white chalk

1 Paint the entire party favor tray with chalkboard spray paint. Let the paint dry completely. Paint the outer border of the party tray using red acrylic paint and allow that paint to dry.

2 Paint the inner border of the tray using green acrylic paint. Allow the paint to dry.

3 Accent the raised areas of the outer border with white acrylic paint and let the paint dry.

4 Tone down the red, white and green painted areas of the tray using brown ink. Using a sanding block, sand the raised areas of the tray until some of the silver shows on the raised portions.

5 Use your finger to rub glitter glue into the recessed areas of the tray. Let the glitter glue dry.

6 Using a strong liquid adhesive, accent the tray with miniature candy canes, holly leaves and baker's twine. Glue a length of baker's twine to the back of the tray to use as a hanger.

   After the chalkboard paint has dried for 24 hours, prime it by rubbing white chalk all over the chalkboard paint, then wipe it off. Once the paint has been primed, you can write a name or message on the tag with chalk.

Cupcake Liner Reflector

I remember lying by my grandparents' Christmas tree with my brother when I was three or four years old. We marveled at how shiny and bright the lights were. Each light had a foil reflector in silver, blue, green, gold or red. The memory of those lights on Grammy and Grampa's tree is the inspiration behind creating these foil light reflectors. I think they are beautiful and add the same shiny, bright glow I remember from my childhood.

Supplies: shadow box, chipboard snowflakes, chipboard banner, mini chipboard frame, mini crown, wooden bingo number, ink (Maya Road); patterned paper (The Girls' Paperie); chipboard buttons, paint, calendar page, mini bingo cards (Jenni Bowlin); plastic bells, sisal wreath and tree (Hobby Lobby); cupcake liners, dove (Wilton); jingle bell (Darice); fine silver German glass glitter (German Corner LLC); gloss medium (Ranger); punches (EK Success); rhinestones (Doodlebug Design Inc.); vintage Santas (Laura's Vintage Garden); other: tags, stickers, leaf pick, deer, miniature clothespins, Scrabble pieces

What You'll Need

silver foil cupcake liners, scissors, wooden bingo piece, strong liquid adhesive

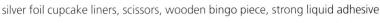

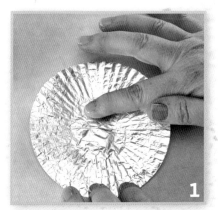

1 Using your fingers, smooth 2 silver foil cupcake liners completely flat.

2 Fold a flattened liner in half 4 times. Using scissors, snip the top portion of the liner to form an upside-down V. Fold and cut the second liner in the same manner.

3 Unfold the liners and check that you like their appearance. Each cut liner should have 16 points.

4 Scrunch the center of 1 liner inward to make it a bit smaller than the other. Attach the smaller liner onto the middle of the larger one using a strong liquid adhesive.

Attach a wooden bingo piece onto the center of the liners with a strong liquid adhesive and scrunch the foil liners around the bingo piece.

More Delightful Options

There are plenty of ways that you can customize the look of your own reflectors. If you prefer fewer points, fold the liners only 3 times instead of 4. Your reflector will have 8 points like the one you see on the right.

It's also easy to color your reflectors. Once the reflector is cut, cover it with alcohol ink in whatever color you prefer. Using red, as I am here, adds to the festive look of this reflector.

Interactive Layers

I remember receiving Christmas cards as a child that had Santa waving his arm when you pulled on a little tab. I always loved these interactive cards. So, when I saw this patterned paper I instantly knew I wanted to use it to make an interactive card of my own. I picked two images from the patterned paper that I thought would complement each other and began to work on my design. I really liked how the one Santa had the doll in his hands and decided this would be the one to overlap the other. Then to add even more holiday cheer, I accented the card using glitter glue and coarse glitter.

Supplies: patterned paper (Pink Paislee); paint (Jenni Bowlin, Ranger); ink (Clearsnap, Ranger); stamps (Wendy Vecchi, The Girls' Paperie); glitter (EK Success); glitter glue (Ranger); decoupage medium (Aleene's); felt (CPE); decorative scissors (Fiskars); trinket pins, velvet trim, chipboard frame (Maya Road); other: cardstock, vintage buttons, lace flower

What You'll Need
images with figures, craft knife, cutting mat, distressing tool, ink, glitter glue

1 Evaluate your images to determine what parts would be best for layering. Look for small parts that extend from the main image. For my card, I thought the waving arm of the Santa image was perfect. Using a craft knife, trim all around the portion of the image you want to layer.

2 Alter the images by using a distressing tool on each edge of the image. Ink the edges of each image.

3 Layer the second image together with the first. If you want to make the layering obvious, you can bend the cut piece upward a bit or elevate it with a foam square.

4 If you desire, accent the images using glitter glue.

More Delightful Options

To make the arm on the Santa moveable, carefully cut the entire arm off and attach it back onto the Santa using a small brad in a matching color. Now you have an arm that is completely interactive.

nbellished Clear Button

ing clear buttons is a great way to customize your project; it allows you to turn a clear button into one that perfectly sorizes your project. Try using patterned papers, vintage ledger paper, book pages or sheet music to transform a button. I used sheet music to embellish clear buttons. I felt this fit nicely with the theme of the project because it reminded me ristmas carols. I added other personal touches to this project as well. For example, the white trim on each mitten was red by a pair of mittens I had when I was little. Oh, how I loved those mittens! I also added extra sparkle throughout the ct to resemble holiday lights sparkling at night. Use details like these to make your projects magical.

Supplies: patterned paper (3ndypapir.no); double-stitched velvet trim, chipboard mittens, ink, chipboard snowflakes, satin pleat trim, glitter, star pin, trinket pin (Maya Road); marabou (Zucker Feather Products); glitter glue, gloss medium (Ranger); jewels (Doodlebug Design Inc.); ink (Clearsnap); button (Autumn Leaves); jingle bell (Westrim Crafts); bead garland (Jo-Ann Fabric and Craft Stores); other: vintage sheet music, seam binding, baker's twine

What You'll Need

clear button, gloss medium, patterned paper, paper piercer, craft knife, cutting mat, sanding block, baker's twine, seam binding

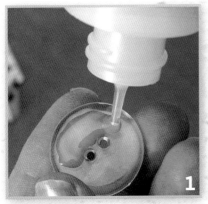

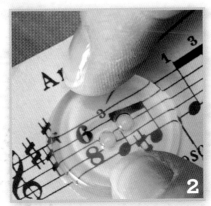

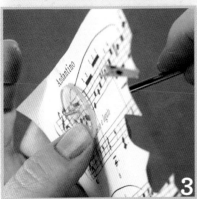

1 Apply gloss medium to the back of a clear button.

2 Place the button, glue side down, onto patterned paper. Here, I'm using vintage sheet music. Press down on the button with medium pressure to remove air bubbles.

3 While the gloss medium is still wet, use a paper piercer to clear each button hole. Let the gloss medium dry completely.

4 Using a craft knife, cut the paper around the button.

5 Sand the edges of the patterned paper until it is smooth and flush with the button.

6 Thread baker's twine through the button holes and tie it into a bow. Create a bow from seam binding and attach the altered button to the center of the seam binding bow.

More Delightful Options

If you want to display these mittens all winter long, change the red and green color scheme to blue and white.

Vintage Photo Vignette

The design for this layout allows you to tell a story with photos and would work beautifully with many themes. I think it would work especially well as a baby layout; you could incorporate a photo taken each month to show the growth or milestones of a new baby. It would also be wonderful for showcasing photos taken from around your home to document special holiday decorations and treats.

Supplies: patterned paper (Pink Paislee); chipboard letters, chipboard snowflakes, ink (Maya Road); ink (Clearsnap); gloss medium (Ranger); fine silver German glass glitter (German Corner LLC); felt (CPE); tiny alphas (Making Memories); self-adhesive pearls (The Paper Studio); chandelier bead (Laura's Vintage Garden); other: vintage ledger paper

What You'll Need

black-and-white photos with a similar theme, laser printer or copier, cardstock, paper trimmer, sewing machine and thread, distressing tool, ink, patterned paper

1 Copy (or scan and print) several black-and-white photos that have a similar theme onto medium-weight white cardstock. I find that using black-and-white photos makes the photos look more cohesive, so if you only have color photos, I suggest converting them to black-and-white. There are several free programs that will do this for you (I use Picasa Web Albums). Trim the photos so they are all the same size (mine are 2" [5cm] squares).

2 Using a sewing machine, sew a straight stitch approximately ⅛" (3mm) inside each edge of each photo. Distress the edges of each photo with a distressing tool or by gently running your fingernail down each edge.

3 Apply ink to the edges of each photo.

4 Cut, sew, distress and ink pieces of patterned paper as you did the photos. Arrange the photos and patterned paper pieces so that the photos tell the story of your chosen layout theme. Once you have found a composition that you like, you can transfer the photos and patterned papers onto a layout.

More Delightful Options

I embellished this layout with chipboard and felt snowflakes. I added self-adhesive pearls to the felt snowflakes for that "something special." For a different look, you could embroider the snowflakes using a backstitch and cream-colored embroidery floss.

Vintage Keepsake Inspiration

The inspiration for this layout came from a letter my grandfather wrote to my grandmother when they were dating. There are so many ways you can use a vintage keepsake to inspire your own layout. For instance, I pulled quotes directly from the letter to embellish the layout, and the scanned image of the envelope the letter was sent in features prominently in the layout. To add to the sweetness of the feeling of this project, I used soft colors, doily patterned paper and plenty of glitter. I feel like the elements I used help tell the story of this love letter perfectly.

Supplies: patterned paper (Pink Paislee); glitter glue, pearlescent pigment powder, pearlescent pigment spray, ink (Ranger); felt (CPE); kraft tag, mini banner stamp, doily stamp (Maya Road); pearls (The Paper Studio); decorative scissors (Fiskars); ink (Clearsnap); alphabet stickers (Adornit); other: baker's twine, seam binding, vintage button

What You'll Need

love letter or other vintage keepsake, scanner, laser printer, cardstock, paper trimmer, patterned paper, craft knife, cutting mat, ink, glue stick, glitter glue

1 Find a love letter or other keepsake that inspires you! Then examine the keepsake for items you can use in your layout. I loved the envelope from my grandfather's love letter, so I knew I wanted to feature it prominently. I scanned the envelope and printed the scanned image onto medium-weight white cardstock using a laser printer. You can easily have a color copy made instead, if you do not have a scanner or laser printer. Use a paper trimmer to trim the cardstock to the size that best fits your project.

2 Use a craft knife to cut out decorative elements from patterned paper.

3 Ink the edges of both your scanned image and patterned papers using brown ink. Attach the patterned papers to the cardstock with a glue stick.

4 Embellish the patterned paper with glitter glue.

More Delightful Options

Here are some more examples of elements I pulled from my grandfather's love letter to use in my layout. I loved that he always started his letters with "My Dearest Girly," and ended them with "P.S. Wrote with a hug sealed with a kiss I love the one that opened this." I highlighted these two sentiments with romantic fonts. I also incorporated a little bit of nature into the design since the photo of my grandmother was taken outside; the bird and butterfly carry the sentiments on this page.

Paint and Ink Patina

While working on this banner, I decided the birds needed to have an aged feel, but I wanted a unique look, different from what you get when an embellishment is covered with old book pages, sheet music or glass glitter. I didn't feel these types of altering would really add to this project. I wanted each bird to have some color but not the typical Valentine color scheme of red, white and pink—I figured that was just too expected. I started to notice a little pop of blue in each of the button images. That is what inspired me to try a patina—a brown tone accented with blue. I think this effect worked out perfectly as the birds have an aged feel with a little pop of color, which is exactly what I wanted.

Supplies: chipboard banner, chipboard birds, chipboard hearts, hanging chandelier beads (Maya Road); paint, buttons (Jenni Bowlin); die-cut lace tags, glitter (EK Success); ink (Clearsnap, Jenni Bowlin, Ranger); pearls (Mark Richards); glitter glue (Ranger); alcohol ink marker (Copic Ciao); fine glass glitter (German Corner LLC); jump rings (Hirschberg Schutz & Co.); chipboard alphabet (The Girls' Paperie); stamp set (Studio 490 by Wendy Vecchi); other: vintage sheet music, baker's twine, seam binding, flocked flowers

What You'll Need

chipboard bird, acrylic paint (two colors), ink, stamp, dimensional adhesive, fine glass glitter

1 Paint a chipboard bird with cream acrylic paint. Let the paint dry completely.

2 Ink the stamp with brown ink, then press the inked stamp on top of the painted chipboard bird. Let the ink dry.

3 Lightly tap a blue paint dabber on top of the painted and inked chipboard bird. Let the paint dry.

4 Cover the entire bird using dimensional adhesive. While the glaze is still wet, sprinkle on a light dusting of fine glass glitter. Allow the glaze to dry.

More Delightful Options

I wanted additional color to be pulled downward on this banner, so I decided to color the chandelier beads using a Copic marker. This is a very simple way to accent any clear glass or acrylic embellishment. If you decide you don't like the color, it can easily be removed with an alcohol swab.

chapter two

Spring

The first sign of spring around our house is when we hear the sparrows singing away while they tidy up the nest they made under the eaves of our garage. The sparrows have been coming back to the same nest for twelve years, so I've watched many a bird family being raised right outside my window. Nothing says spring like watching the babies take their first flight. As spring progresses, the flowers all start to bloom. We have to enjoy the flowers quickly because the rabbits in the neighborhood feast on them as they bloom. Getting to see all the adorable baby bunnies playing or hiding in the bushes makes up for never having flowers last for more than a day.

Spring is filled with beautiful pastels, the sweet sounds of nature and the feeling of a fresh new start. In this chapter, I will show you how to take all the different aspects of spring and use them in your projects. For example, on page 44, I'll show you how to embellish simple silk flowers with Copic markers and a little glitter so they're just as beautiful as the spring flowers in your garden. I'll also show you how to create your own flowers with diverse materials, including fabric, modeling film and buttons. You can use these techniques to embellish projects to celebrate spring itself, or to commemorate the wonderful holidays of spring, including Easter, Mother's Day and Father's Day.

As you watch all the signs of spring happen before your eyes, take note of nature's beautiful, soft color palette and use it as inspiration for your projects. The soft colors and textures of spring are perfect for the pretty vintage style I'll share here with you.

Paper Cone Medallion

The inspiration for this spring ornament came from one of my favorite old-fashioned flowers—the foxglove. Each cone around the edge of the ornament represents a bloom on this beautiful plant. I decided to accent the center of each cone using a pearl stick pin because of the added interest and shine each pin gives to the ornament. The other elements that help bring this project together are the double bow and the resin flower. Using two colors of seam binding in the double bow helped balance the color scheme and toned down all the green, while the resin flower in the center of the bow finished the project off perfectly.

Supplies: chipboard base, pearl pins, resin flower (Maya Road); patterned paper (The Girls' Paperie); punch, decorative scissors (Fiskars); vintage image (Crafty Secrets); ink (Clearsnap); glitter glue (Ranger); self-adhesive pearls (The Paper Studio); glitter (EK Success); rhinestones (Heidi Swapp); tiny alphas (Making Memories); other: seam binding, silk flowers

What You'll Need

chipboard piece, patterned paper, glue stick, craft knife, cutting mat, sanding block, ink, extra-large scallop square punch, large scallop square punch, liquid adhesive, decorative pearl pins, wire cutters, hot glue gun, glitter glue

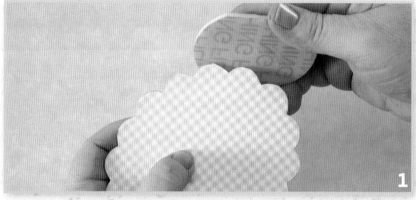

1 Adhere a scalloped oval chipboard piece to a piece of patterned paper using a glue stick. Use a craft knife to trim the paper around the chipboard. Sand the edges of the piece smooth. Ink the edges of the chipboard piece.

2 Using an extra-large scallop square punch (about 1½"), punch 16 scallop squares from the patterned paper. Do the same with a large scallop square punch (about 1¼").

3 Pinch a punched paper square at one point to begin rounding the paper into a cone.

4 Hold the square with the pinched point at the bottom, then fold the left and right points towards each other. Secure the edges to one another with a liquid adhesive. Repeat this step on all the scallop squares. Allow the glue to dry.

5 Place the cones made from the extra-large scallop squares side by side around the edge of the chipboard base with the patterned paper on the chipboard facing down. Once you have the cones arranged as you like, attach them to the chipboard base with a liquid adhesive.

6 Place the cones made from the large scallop squares on top of the extra-large scallop square cones, nestling them so the large cones lay where two extra-large cones join. Once you have them arranged as you like, attach them to the base with a liquid adhesive as well.

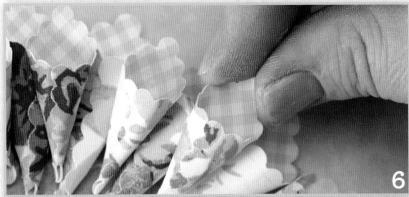

7 Using wire cutters, snip the sharp ends off the pearl pins. Slide a pearl pin into each extra-large scallop square cone.

8 Once all the pins are in place, use a hot glue gun to secure the tips of the pins to the chipboard base.

More Delightful Options

This medallion would look nice as an embellishment for the front of an album or even placed in a frame as a piece of holiday art.

9 Insert a pin into a large scallop square cone. Trim off any excess length from the pin using wire cutters. Remove the pin from the cone, add a dot of adhesive to the end and put the pin back in the cone. Repeat with each large cone. Allow the glue to dry.

10 Accent the scallops of each cone with glitter glue. Here, I used Diamond Stickles.

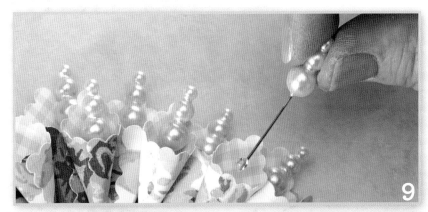

More Project Details

I thought the image of this little girl in her spring outfit, holding the tulip with the duckling at her feet, was so cute. Once I placed the image in the middle, I felt it needed a bit more impact. So, I took an exact copy of the image and cut it out using a craft knife. Next, I placed foam squares onto the back of the cutout image and attached it directly on top of the first image. I accented the collar, sleeves and buttons on her outfit using Diamond Stickles. Having the added sparkle and dimension completed this project perfectly.

Scalloped Paper Fringe

The photo on the front of this card is one of my favorites. It shows my dad with his sisters and brother one Easter Sunday. The original photo was in full color, but I felt the colors clashed a bit with the patterned papers I wanted to use, so I printed the photo in black and white. To capture the holiday spirit, and inspired by the feeling of spring emerging after a cold New Hampshire winter, I decided to accent this card with brightly colored patterned papers, paper butterflies, tiny paper flowers, hand-cut leaves and a cute scallop fringe I created to replicate the beautiful color of fresh spring grass.

Wishing You A Happy Easter

Supplies: patterned paper (Jenni Bowlin, October Afternoon); ink (Clearsnap); decorative scissors (Fiskars); punch (EK Success); velvet rickrack, gingham (Maya Road); self-adhesive pearls (The Paper Studio); glitter glue (Ranger); other: paper flowers, baker's twine

What You'll Need

patterned paper, paper trimmer, scallop scissors, straight scissors, ink, glue stick, glitter glue, gingham trim, fabric adhesive, velvet rickrack, paper flowers, strong liquid adhesive, butterfly punch

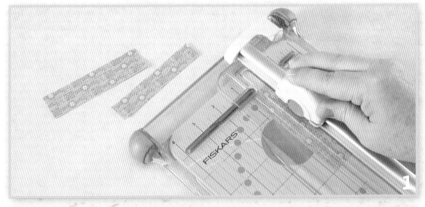

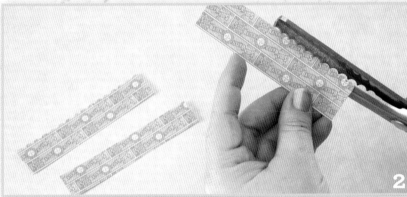

1 Using a paper trimmer, cut 3 strips of patterned paper. The strips should be as wide as your project (here, a card); the first strip should be 1" (3cm) tall, the second should be ¾" (2cm) tall and the third should be ½" (13mm) tall.

2 Trim 1 long edge of each strip with scallop scissors.

3 Using straight-edge scissors, make ¼" (6mm) cuts between each scallop on all 3 patterned paper strips.

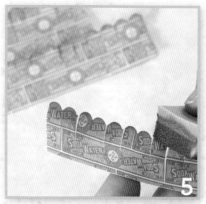

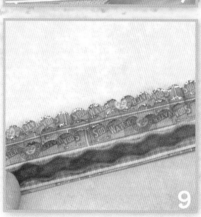

4 Use your thumb to gently curl the scallop fringe downward on each paper strip.

5 Ink the edges of each paper strip using brown ink.

6 Using a glue stick, attach the ¾" (2cm) strip on top of the 1" (3cm) strip with the bottom edges aligned; attach the ½" (13mm) to the ¾" (2cm) in the same manner.

7 Accent the scallops using glitter glue (I used Platinum Stickles). Let the glitter glue dry completely.

8 Using fabric adhesive, attach a piece of gingham trim to the bottom of the ½" (13mm) piece of paper.

9 Attach a piece of velvet rickrack to the middle of the gingham trim with fabric adhesive.

10 Accent the paper fringe by attaching paper flowers with a strong liquid adhesive.

11 Punch a few small butterflies out of patterned paper and attach them to the fringe using a strong liquid adhesive.

More Project Details

I created the Easter egg photo frame on this card by using a playing card that my daughters had when they were younger as a template. I cut out an oval in the center of the card where I wanted the photo to go. Once I had the egg template, I traced it onto white cardstock and cut it out. Next, I layered patterned paper strips onto the egg, attaching them with a glue stick. Using a sewing machine, I sewed a straight stitch along the inner edge of the outer portion of the egg and the inner edge of the inside oval section of the egg. Where the patterned papers meet, I stitched using a zigzag stitch. I then distressed the inner and outer edges of the egg and inked them using a creamy brown ink. To accent the egg, I applied strips of 5mm self-adhesive cream-colored pearls onto the patterned paper.

Fabric Strip Flower

This fun flower brings together a great variety of textures and colors, so it is the perfect way to draw all of the elements of your project together. On my card, I used fabrics of three different textures—smooth, matte cotton; fuzzy chenille; and shiny satin. These texture changes draw together the matte and shine of different elements in the card. I drew together the colors of the card in this flower as well. The cotton strips at the bottom of the flower reflect the blues of the patterned papers I chose, while the creamy chenille and satin enhance the warm, cream tones in the vintage book pages and doilies I chose. For an added special touch, add a pinback to the fabric strip flower and attach it to the card using the pin. The card's recipient can then remove the flower from the card and wear it proudly!

Supplies: patterned paper (Pink Paislee); chipboard butterfly, chipboard letters, kraft doily, satin pleat trim, ink, pins (Maya Road); decorative scissors (Fiskars); self-adhesive pearls (The Paper Studio); ink (Clearsnap); pearlescent pigment spray, gloss medium, glitter glue (Ranger); other: fabric, book page, Copic marker

What You'll Need

fabric remnants (two colors), paper trimmer, fabric adhesive, satin pleat trim, scissors, self-adhesive pearl

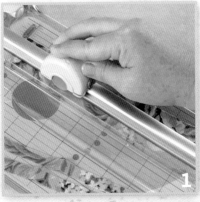

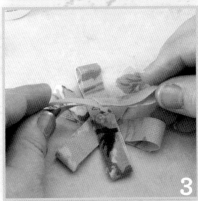

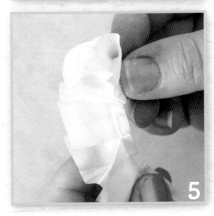

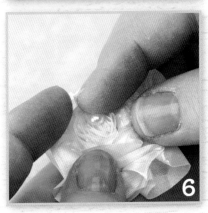

1 Cut 10 strips of fabric, all the same color, to ½" × 4" (13mm × 10cm). Cut 5 strips of fabric in a second color to ¼" × 3" (6mm × 8cm).

2 Place a small amount of fabric adhesive on the center of each fabric strip. Fold both ends toward the center and place them into the adhesive.

3 Add a small amount of fabric adhesive to the center of one fabric loop. Place another fabric loop on top to create an X.

4 Continue attaching fabric strips to the stack, rotating them to fill in the gaps. Randomly mix the fabrics.

5 Once all the fabric strips have been attached to each other, cut a 12" (30cm) length of satin pleat trim. Begin rolling the trim at one end.

6 Continue to roll the trim until you reach the end. (The size of the flower will be determined by the length of your trim. If your flower is too large for your taste, cut off the excess satin pleat trim.) Secure the end of the satin pleat trim to the rest of the flower with a drop of fabric adhesive. Attach a self-adhesive pearl to the center of the satin flower. Glue the satin flower to the top of the fabric strip flower.

Embellished Silk Flower

Altering silk flowers is one way to take a simple inexpensive silk flower and turn it into a gorgeous embellishment for any project. Using Copic Markers is one of my favorite ways to do this. These markers come in many different shades and are easy to use. And applying glitter to silk flowers gives them a beautiful dewy frosted look. Look in thrift stores for bunches of small white or cream-colored silk flower bunches (they're the easiest to alter). Don't worry about the condition you find them in, especially if you are a vintage girl at heart, because tattered and frayed edges make them even better.

Supplies: patterned paper (Little Yellow Bicycle); paint (Jenni Bowlin); chipboard frames (Maya Road); distress crackle paint, glitter glue (Ranger); tiny alphas (Making Memories); self-adhesive pearls (The Paper Studio); ink (Clearsnap); punch, glitter (EK Success); vintage images (Crafty Secrets); decoupage medium (iLoveToCreate); leaves (Laura's Vintage Garden); other: Copic markers, trim, silk flowers, seam binding

What You'll Need
silk flowers, Copic markers (five colors), decoupage medium, paintbrush, coarse crystal glitter, tweezers, strong liquid adhesive, self-adhesive pearls, silk leaves, glitter glue, fabric adhesive

1 Remove the petal portion of the silk flower from the stem. Separate the petal layers.

2 Using Copic markers in several different colors, randomly color the silk flower pieces.

3 Use a paintbrush to apply decoupage medium to the flower pieces.

4 While the decoupage medium is still wet, generously sprinkle coarse crystal glitter over the flower pieces. Allow the decoupage medium to dry.

5 Use a strong liquid adhesive to attach the petal layers to each other.

6 Color a 5mm self-adhesive pearl with a Copic marker. Allow the ink to dry.

7 Attach the pearl to the center of the flower. Use tweezers to reach inside the flower if necessary.

8 Apply glitter glue to the top of the colored pearl and to the edges of each flower petal. Using a fabric adhesive, attach 2 silk leaves to the bottom of the flower.

More Delightful Options
I made this tag for Easter, but with a few changes, it could be attached to a baby shower gift. Just change the sentiment to one that fits the occasion. For a more personalized tag, you could use photos of the mom- and dad-to-be when they were babies, instead of the clip art I used. This would certainly be a cherished piece that could be framed and placed in the new baby's nursery.

Modeling Film Flower

Modeling film is a really fun product to play with; you can cut it into any shape with decorative scissors or dies, then use a heat gun to shape it into unique embellishments. Keep this product in mind when you look at dies, especially flower dies. You could create an entire bouquet of these flowers by using several different flower dies. When you are creating flowers, you do need to work quickly once you turn off the heat gun as the film cools down fast, and once it is cooled, the film hardens into shape. However, if a petal is not quite how you want it, just reheat and reshape. Remember to work safely, as the heat gun is very hot and you don't want to burn yourself!

Supplies: coaster album, chipboard scroll (Maya Road); dies (Sizzix); modeling film, stamp (Studio 490 by Wendy Vecchi); ink (Ranger, Clearsnap, Maya Road); paint (Jenni Bowlin); fine silver German glass glitter (German Corner LLC); distress glitter glue, glitter glue, ultra thick embossing enamel, alcohol ink (Ranger); stamens (Wilton); felt (CPE); decorative scissors (Fiskars); leaves (Laura's Vintage Garden); other: vintage sheet music

What You'll Need

modeling film, large flower die, alcohol inks (three colors), alcohol ink blending tool, nonstick craft mat, stamp, acrylic block, ink, scissors, heat tool, strong, clear-drying liquid adhesive, silk flower stamens and leaves, glitter glue

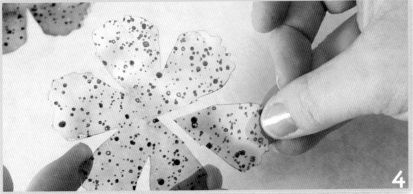

1 Using a large flower die, cut 3 flowers out of modeling film (I used the Tattered Floral Bigz Die for my die and Clearly For Art for my modeling film). Place the die-cut flowers onto a nonstick craft mat and apply the alcohol inks. I blended 3 alcohol ink colors on the flowers by applying the inks directly to the felt part of a blending tool and rotating the blending tool after each application.

2 Apply ink to a texture stamp and stamp each flower.

3 Cut between 2 petals to the center of one of the flowers. (Later we'll refer to this as Flower 1.)

4 Repeat step 3 on a second flower. Make a second cut on this flower to completely remove 1 petal. (Later we'll refer to this as Flower 2.)

More Delightful Options

The cover of this album would make a beautiful accent for the top of a decorative box or even a piece of framed art.

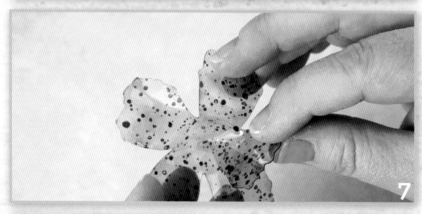

5 Repeat step 3 on the last flower. Make a second cut to remove 2 joined petals from this flower. The larger piece with 4 petals is Flower 3 and the smaller piece with 2 petals is Flower 4.

6 Using the heat tool, heat Flower 1. While the modeling film is soft, mold the flower so that the petal on the right side of the cut you made is on top of the petal to the left side of the cut. Drawing the flower together in this way will give it somewhat of a cone shape and will make the piece dimensional. Let the modeling film cool completely.

7 Repeat step 6 with Flower 2. Since one of the petals has been removed from Flower 2, it will form a smaller cone than Flower 1.

8 Repeat step 6 with Flower 3.

9 Using the heat tool, heat Flower 4 and roll it into a small cone. If desired, you can clip the petals in half to make them a bit smaller and more delicate looking.

10 Using a strong, clear-drying liquid adhesive, attach the flower pieces. Stack them largest to smallest. Let the glue dry completely.

11 Attach silk flower stamens into the center of the flower using a clear-drying adhesive. Accent the edges of each petal using glitter glue. Allow the glitter glue to dry completely.

12 Attach 2 silk leaves underneath the flower using a strong liquid adhesive.

More Delightful Options

If modeling film isn't your medium of choice, you can also create this gorgeous flower using fabric scraps and fabric stiffener. Cut the fabric pieces exactly as you would modeling film, but once they're cut, soak them in fabric stiffener. Then, while the stiffener is still wet, shape the petals as shown here. You will need to be inventive to find ways to make the petals stay in shape while they dry. Try propping them up with glasses and other kitchen items. Once dry, use a fabric adhesive to attach the pieces into a stack.

There is always more than one way to do something to make it fit your taste, especially in the crafting world. Always experiment!

Felt Message Banner

I always have a hard time finding something to give my mom for Mother's Day—the woman has everything! If you have the same problem, try creating something unique just for your mom; that's what I did with this project. Since my mom loves anything vintage (now you know where I get it from), I altered the spool and flowers in this sculpture using vintage sheet music that we found together in an antique store. I then created flowers from old book pages to accent the bobbins. Finally, I stitched a personal sentiment onto a felt banner and wrapped it around the spool. These special touches make this a unique Mother's Day gift.

Supplies: spool (Studio 490 by Wendy Vecchi); adhesive (iLoveToCreate); glitter, punch (EK Success); felt (CPE); embroidery floss (DMC); ink (Clearsnap); stamens (Wilton); wool roving (Clover); die (Sizzix); decorative scissors (Fiskars); glitter glue (Ranger); crochet trim (Maya Road); other: nest, eggs, birds, bobbin, seam binding, vintage ledger, music sheets, book pages

What You'll Need

felt, paper trimmer, scallop scissors, straight scissors, disappearing fabric pen, embroidery floss, sewing needle, seam binding, fabric adhesive, fabric remnants, flower die, buttons

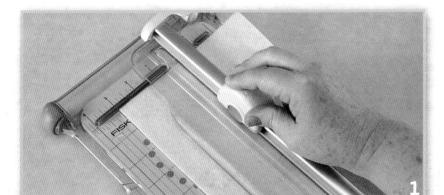

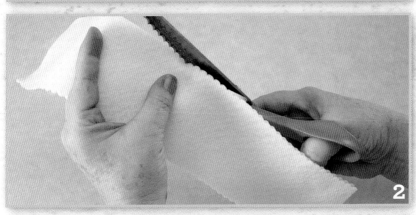

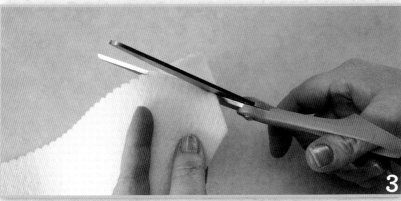

1 Using a paper trimmer, cut 2 pieces of felt to 3" × 12" (8cm × 30cm).

2 Holding the pieces of felt together, trim the long edges with scallop scissors.

3 Trim the corners off of the right side of the felt pieces. Trim all 3 edges at this end using scallop scissors.

4 Using a disappearing fabric pen, write your sentiment on the felt. Draw a heart on each end.

More Delightful Options

This project would also make a wonderful wedding gift—just stitch the bride and groom's monograms or wedding date onto the felt.

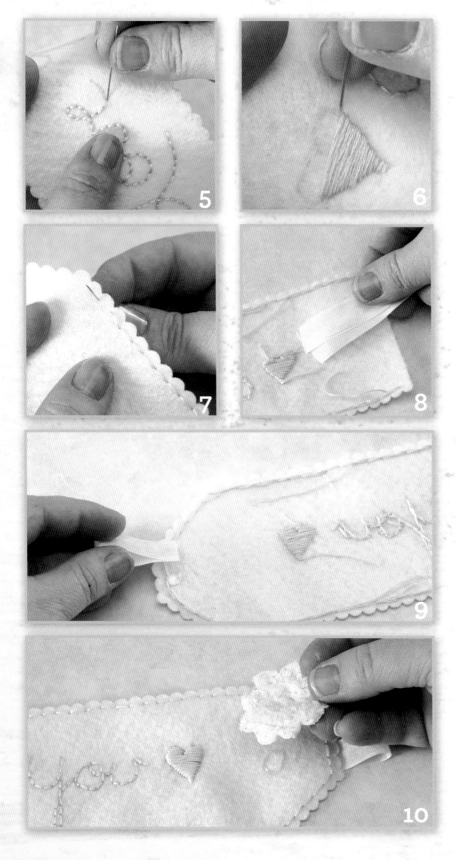

5 Thread a sewing needle with 3 strands of embroidery floss and begin stitching along the sentiment with a backstitch. Continue until the entire sentiment has been embroidered.

6 Next, fill in each drawn heart with a satin stitch.

7 Sew along the scallop edges of the felt piece using a backstitch.

8 Cut 2 pieces of seam binding, each 12" (30cm) long. Use fabric adhesive to attach both to the back of the stitched piece of felt at the center of the left edge (the edge without the corners cut off). You'll use these pieces to tie the banner to the project.

9 Cut 1 piece of seam binding 3" (3cm) long, fold it in half and, using fabric adhesive, attach it to the back of the stitched piece of felt at the center of the right edge.

10 Using a flower die, cut 1 flower from a remnant of fabric. Attach the flower to the right end of the banner next to a stitched heart using fabric adhesive.

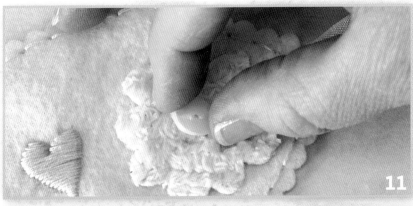

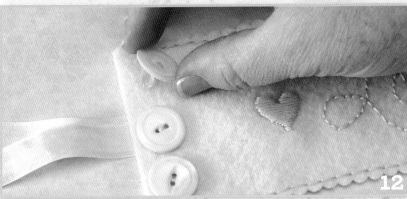

11 Thread embroidery floss through the holes of a single button. Secure the thread with a knot. Attach the button to the center of the fabric flower using fabric adhesive.

12 Accent the left end of the banner with 3 buttons that have been threaded with embroidery floss; attach them to the felt using fabric adhesive. Use fabric adhesive to attach the second piece of felt to the back of the first piece of felt. Once all of the fabric adhesive dries, the banner is ready to be added to a project.

More Project Details

I wanted to add some height to this piece between the top of the spool base and the nest, so I started digging in my supplies to find just the right thing. What made my search even more difficult was the fact that I wanted whatever I used to add some color as well. I considered using spools wrapped with fabric and embroidery floss, but I could not get the height just right using multiple spools. Then I found some thread-filled bobbins that I had been saving for just the right project. Stacking two of the bobbins on top of each other created exactly the look I wanted—I now had the proper height and some pops of color. If you can't find vintage bobbins, you can use modern metal bobbins or clear plastic bobbins filled with thread in a color that will complement your project. This is a really unique and fun way to accent your projects.

Decorative Book Binding

I've always loved the spines of vintage books; they have so much personality. With this technique, you can create your own one-of-a-kind decorative book binding for the spines of mini albums or journals. With so many wonderful stamp images available, there is no end to the designs you can create, and while I used ink to alter the color of the binding, you can use paint or mists instead to achieve the color you want. This technique is an easy one to experiment with to really make a project your own.

Supplies: album, spray ink, chipboard alphas, crocheted trim, chipboard butterfly, chipboard alphas (Maya Road); ink, paint (Jenni Bowlin); pearlescent pigment powder, pearlescent pigment spray, glitter glue, gloss medium, paint, gel medium, Perfect Medium (Ranger); ink, distress crackle paint, decorative scissors (Fiskars); decoupage medium (iLoveToCreate); die (Sizzix); hinging tape (Lineco); stamp (Studio 490 by Wendy Vecchi); buttons (Advantus); glitter (EK Success); embroidery floss (DMC); other: cheesecloth, tissue paper, glitter, vintage buttons

What You'll Need

self-adhesive linen hinging tape, scissors, photo album or book, scallop scissors, ink (two colors), script stamp, buttons, embroidery floss, fabric adhesive

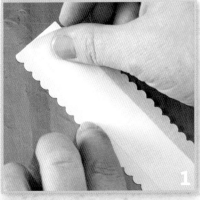

1 Cut a piece of self-adhesive linen hinging tape that is long enough to cover the spine of your album. Depending on the width of the spine, you may need more than 1 piece of tape. For my album, I needed 2. Using scallop scissors, trim the long edges of the linen hinging tape (if you are using 2 pieces as I did, only trim 1 long edge on each piece).

If you are using more than 1 piece of linen hinging tape, remove the paper backing from 1 piece. Overlap this piece with the other to make a piece of binding wide enough to cover the spine of your album.

2 Apply ink over the entire surface of the piece or pieces of tape. For a vintage look, use brown ink.

3 Apply ink to a script stamp and stamp the image onto the tape. Use the stamp again if needed to cover the entire piece of binding.

4 Thread embroidery floss through the holes of a single button. Secure the thread with a knot. Attach the button to the center of the binding using fabric adhesive. Repeat to create a line of buttons along the entire length of the binding. (The hinging tape is self-adhesive. To apply the decorative binding to your album or book, simply peel and stick.)

More Project Details

For the background of this mini album, I wanted a subtle amount of texture. After painting the cover with acrylic paint, I decided to place a thin layer of cheesecloth on top of the paint. I then secured the cheesecloth to the album using a thin coating of melted beeswax here and there. After the beeswax cooled off, I lightly inked the cheesecloth with a creamy brown ink. It gave me exactly the texture I was looking for.

Fabric Cabbage Roses

I wanted this layout to have a great vintage feel, and I used lots of different details to create that look. I started with the cabbage roses, which are a sweet, old-fashioned flower. I used vintage fabrics to give the flowers even more classic appeal. The red and green patterned papers I chose shared the sweet look of the flowers, while the great black-and-white paper added the look of a vintage newspaper page. I also used the title and journaling to reinforce the look I was going for. I started with the larger bingo letters, which I distressed and inked, then I inked the edges of the journaling strips as well. I feel these little touches help bring the vintage feel of the layout together.

Supplies: patterned paper (October Afternoon); glitter glue (Ranger); ink (Clearsnap); decorative scissors (Fiskars); leaf pins (Maya Road); self-adhesive pearls (The Paper Studio); alpha tiles (Jenni Bowlin); tiny alphas (Making Memories); embroidery floss (DMC); punch (EK Success); other: vintage buttons, fabric

What You'll Need

fabric, paper trimmer, cardstock, fabric adhesive, scissors, self-adhesive pearls, leaf pins

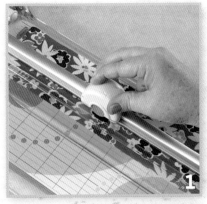

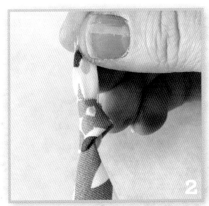

1 Using a paper trimmer, cut a 1" × 18" (3cm × 46cm) strip of fabric.

2 Tie a knot at the end of the fabric strip.

3 Cut a circle of cardstock to serve as the base of the flower. Make the circle the size you want your finished flower to be. Mine is approximately 1½" (4cm) in diameter.

Apply fabric adhesive to the center of the cardstock and place the knotted end into the adhesive. Begin wrapping the fabric strip around the knot, twisting the fabric as you wrap. Continue wrapping and twisting the strip, adding adhesive to the cardstock when needed.

4 Continue twisting and wrapping until you reach the edge of the cardstock. If there is any fabric left when you reach the edge, trim any excess fabric off. Tuck the end of the fabric strip between the cardstock and the last round of wrapped and twisted fabric.

5 Accent the center of the flower with either a single 10mm self-adhesive pearl or with 3 5mm self-adhesive pearls.

6 Place leaf pins into the edge of the flower as an additional embellishment if you desire.

Altered Chipboard Letters

Ultra Thick Embossing Enamel is a great way to add color and texture to plain chipboard letters. You can cover the letters completely with UTEE or just accent the edges as shown in this technique. Using an Embossing Medium Pen makes accenting the edges super easy because you have better control to where you want the UTEE to be applied. That's what I did on this layout honoring my dad and grandpa—they were quite the pair. Whenever Grandpa came to visit for the winter (he preferred our Texas winters to his Maine winters), you could always find him and Dad in the shop tinkering on something.

Supplies: patterned paper, pen nibs, stickers, tiny attacher staples (Tim Holtz); chipboard letters (Heidi Swapp); Perfect Medium Pen, ink, ultra thick embossing enamel, pearlescent pigment spray (Ranger); kraft doily (Maya Road); other: milk bottle cap, vintage button

What You'll Need

chipboard letter, embossing medium pen, ultra thick embossing enamel (UTEE), tweezers, heat tool

1 Using an embossing medium pen, ink the outer edges of a chipboard letter. Work with one small section at a time because the medium dries quickly (if you outline the entire letter, the medium will dry before you can move to the next step).

2 Hold the chipboard letter with tweezers and dip it into the UTEE. (I used gold UTEE.) Tap off the excess UTEE.

3 Holding the chipboard letter securely with tweezers, melt the UTEE with a heat tool. Let the UTEE set. Repeat steps 1–3 to cover all of the edges of the letter.

Button Boutonniere

This card could easily be transformed into a birthday card or a card to celebrate any special occasion. For a more feminine card, turn your boutonniere into a bouquet with brightly colored buttons. With so many different button shapes and colors available, it's easy to customize the look of this project. To finish the transformation from boutonniere to bouquet, instead of a straight pin, accent the lace trim with a small butterfly punched out of patterned paper.

Happy Father's Day

Supplies: patterned paper (BasicGrey); ink (Clearsnap); doily (EK Success); floral wire, floral tape (Fiskars); self-adhesive pearls (The Paper Studio); pearlescent pigment powder, pearlescent pigment spray, paint (Ranger); vintage trim, leaf (Laura's Vintage Garden); other: vintage buttons

What You'll Need

shank buttons, floral wire, wire cutters, floral tape, silk leaf, ink, lace, scissors, pin, self-adhesive pearls

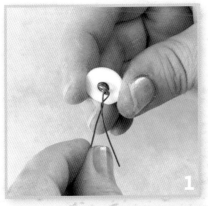

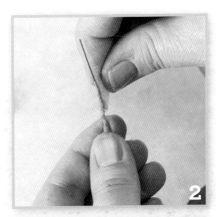

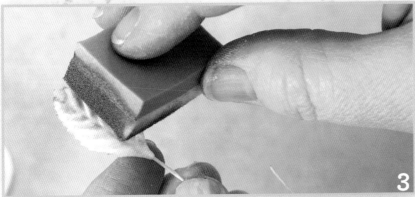

1 Secure the end of a piece of floral wire to the shank of a button. Using wire cutters, trim the wire to the stem length you desire.

2 Wrap the floral wire with floral tape. Start under the button and work toward the free end of the wire.

3 Repeat steps 1 and 2 to create 2 more button "flowers." Vary the stem lengths so that one flower is taller than the others. Distress a silk leaf using brown ink, then attach the leaf to the tallest flower by wrapping the wire on the leaf and the stem of the flower together with floral tape.

4 Arrange the button flowers as you want them. Wrap a piece of lace around the stems and secure with a knot. Place a straight pin through the center of the knot to secure it.

5 Using wire cutters, trim the stems so they are the same length at the bottom. Accent the center of each button with a self-adhesive pearl.

chapter three

Summer

Summer is the time for lazy days, dripping popsicles and more fun with a water hose than a kid could ever imagine. When I was younger, I spent my summer days outside—I was not about to go inside and miss out on all the fun! I especially loved all the bright colors of summer. I can remember as a child being so excited about getting a brightly colored beach ball or pail and shovel; as I got older I'd pick out colorful bathing suits and beach towels. Every summer, my family would go sailing or spend time at the beach. Dad and I always came home sunburned while Mom and my sister and brother ended up as tan as could be. Summer was definitely family time as I was growing up, and with summer came many family birthdays and weddings. In this chapter, I will show you how to celebrate these occasions in special ways.

On page 66, I will show you how to turn a family photo into a precious embellishment for a birthday card. You'll find more birthday fun on pages 70 and 82 as well. I'll also show you how to create beautiful embellishments for wedding cards on pages 72 and 78. Explore this chapter for ideas to commemorate other summery themes, like travel. I hope during your lazy days of summer you have time to experiment with different techniques as I have in this chapter. Summer gives me the freedom to get lost in a project—my new way of enjoying those lazy days of summer. Instead of having sticky hands from drippy popsicles, now my hands are covered in paint, ink and glue.

Grungepaper Rose

As a child I remember walking along the sand dunes with my mom and coming across some flowers that looked just like tiny wooden roses. I have always been intrigued by these and was so happy when I figured out a way to recreate them using Grungepaper, a sturdy but flexible craft material from Tim Holtz. Grungepaper makes creating these flowers much easier since it can be easily rolled and once the petals are bent, they will maintain their shape. Grungepaper can be inked or painted, covered completely in shimmery glitter or accented with Stickles, as I did on my roses. You can alter the roses to match the color scheme for any project.

Supplies: patterned paper (Sassafras Lass); grungepaper (Tim Holtz); paint (Jenni Bowlin); ink, glitter glue, distress glitter glue (Ranger); ink (Clearsnap); chipboard frame (Maya Road); stamp (Wendy Vecchi); die-cut lace tags, glitter (EK Success); punch, decorative scissors (Fiskars); decoupage medium (iLoveToCreate); self-adhesive pearls (The Paper Studio); leaves (Laura's Vintage Garden); other: burlap, vintage button, seam binding

What You'll Need

grungepaper, paper trimmer, scallop scissors, straight scissors, paintbrush, acrylic paint, strong liquid adhesive, ink, glitter glue, felt leaves, fabric adhesive

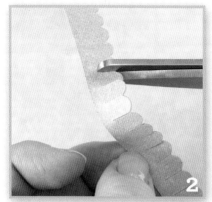

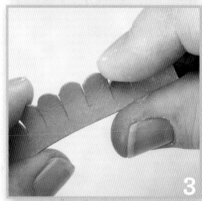

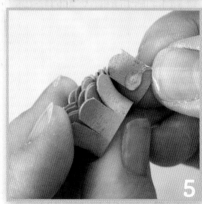

1 Using a paper trimmer, cut a piece of grungepaper to ½" × 12" (13mm × 30cm). Use scallop scissors to trim 1 long edge of the grungepaper.

2 Snip in between each scallop using straight-edge scissors.

3 Paint the grungepaper strip with the color of your choice. Allow the paint to dry completely. With your fingers, bend the petals downward slightly.

4 Curl the end of the grungepaper strip so that the petals bend outward. Begin rolling the grungepaper strip.

5 Continue rolling until the rose is the size you desire. Trim off any excess grungepaper. Apply a strong liquid adhesive to the end of the strip and secure it to the rose.

6 Bend the petals downward again if needed; ink the tips of the petals using brown ink.

7 Accent the tips of the petals with glitter glue. On the orange rose, I used Stickles in Diamond and Distress Stickles in Spiced Marmalade.

8 Using a fabric adhesive, attach felt leaves to the back of the flower.

Family Photo Embellishment

How fun would it be for a family member to receive a card featuring his or her own photo turned into a charming embellishment? I love using old family photos, and this one of my mom is a favorite! One detail I worked in with this card was to make my mom's elbow hang over the birthday greeting banner—this adds dimension and gives the photo a more interactive look on the card. Try accenting the clothing in your photo with patterned paper as I did, or use small pieces of trim or fabric. You can create hats from book pages or patterned paper or attach tiny flowers to create a floral crown. Really, there is no right or wrong way to alter your photos. Just enjoy the creative process!

Supplies: patterned paper (Pink Paislee); clip art (Crafty Secrets); glitter glue, gloss medium (Ranger); chipboard crown, ink (Maya Road); decorative scissors (Fiskars); decoupage medium (iLoveToCreate); glitter (EK Success); fine silver German glass glitter (German Corner LLC); ink (Clearsnap); self-adhesive pearls (The Paper Studio); pearlescent chalks (Pebbles Inc.); other: vintage buttons, baker's twine, vintage sheet music

What You'll Need

family photo, laser printer or copier, cardstock, scissors, pearlescent chalks, chalk applicator, patterned paper (two patterns), scallop scissors, ink, glitter glue, glue stick, self-adhesive pearls, glitter, decoupage medium, chipboard crown, gloss medium, liquid adhesive, craft knife, cutting mat

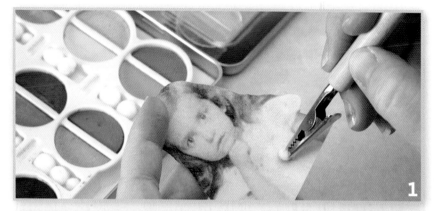

1 Copy (or scan and print) a family photo onto cardstock. Cut out the image you want to embellish for your project. Accent and add color to the image with pearlescent chalks.

2 Create accents to embellish the image. For my image, I created a collar and row of buttons for the dress my mom is wearing in the photo. I cut vintage sheet music using scallop scissors, then embellished the image with brown ink, glitter glue and self-adhesive pearls. Attach the embellishments to the image using a glue stick.

3 Accent the image with glitter glue.

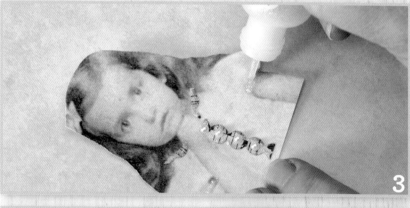

4 Cut a pair of wings from a piece of patterned paper. Apply decoupage medium to each wing, sprinkle glitter over the wings and tap off any excess. Let the decoupage medium dry.

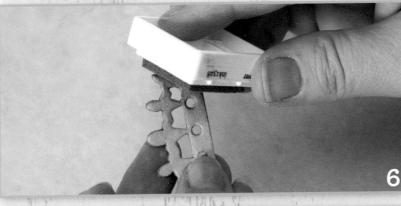

5 Using a glue stick, attach the wings to the back of the photo. Accent the edges of the wings using glitter glue.

6 This image has one last embellishment. To make it, start by applying silver ink to a chipboard crown.

7 Apply gloss medium to the crown and sprinkle it with glitter. I used fine German glass glitter for my crown. Tap off any excess glitter and allow the gloss medium to dry.

8 Accent the crown using self-adhesive pearls.

More Delightful Options

If you wish, you can give a black-and-white photograph a warmer look by reprinting the photo in sepia tones.

9 Attach the altered chipboard crown to the photo using liquid adhesive.

10 If you like, you can alter the image for interactive layering with other elements. Use a craft knife to carefully trim the photo so the sentiment for the card can fit just underneath the cut area.

More Project Details

I wanted a fairy garden feel for this birthday card, so I decided to create my own little flower garden. First, I chose a patterned paper that had flowers of several different sizes. I cut each one out using a craft knife. I arranged the flowers on the background so it would look as though the embellished photo was sitting among the flowers. I inked the edges of each flower using a creamy brown ink, and to add a little sparkle to the flowers, I accented each of the centers using Stickles glitter glue in Diamond.

Decorative Pick

This tower of boxes, decorated to look like a birthday cake, is a very special way to present a birthday gift! This example is for a girl's sixteenth birthday, but you can easily customize this project to fit anyone (or any occasion). Try starting with boxes in different shapes and sizes, such as stars, ovals or squares. Next, select a color scheme that will delight the recipient. Finally, customize your picks, too. Stars or balloons are good choices for a birthday celebration, while storks, rattles or a baby bottle would be perfect for a baby shower.

Supplies: papier mâché boxes, wire, rhinestones (Darice); paint (Jenni Bowlin); chipboard alphas, pleated trim (Maya Road); patterned paper (The Girls' Paperie); glitter glue (Ranger); ink (Clearsnap); decorative scissors (Fiskars); crepe paper (Designware); glitter, punch (EK Success)

What You'll Need

patterned paper, paper punch, 24-gauge wire, wire cutters, strong liquid adhesive, ink, self-adhesive rhinestones, glitter glue, paper piercer

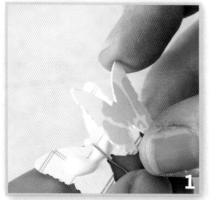

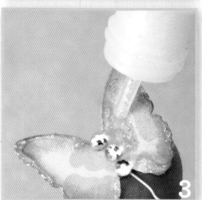

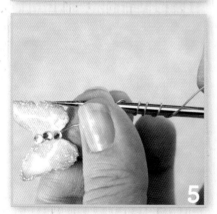

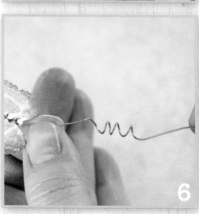

1 Using wire cutters, cut an 8" (20cm) length of 24-gauge wire. Punch 2 butterflies out of patterned paper. Place strong liquid adhesive on the back of a butterfly, place the end of the wire into the center of the adhesive, then place the second butterfly on top of the adhesive, sandwiching the wire in between the butterflies.

2 Ink the edges on both the front and the back of the butterfly.

3 Accent the body of the butterfly using three clear self-adhesive rhinestones on each side. Apply glitter glue to the butterfly as well.

4 Bend and curve the wire of the pick by hand.

5 If you like, you can give your pick a fun detail by coiling the wire. Wrap the wire several times around a paper piercer for a tight coil.

6 Remove the wire from the paper piercer and spread the coils a bit for a more natural look.

Paper Lace Trim

I think the paper lace I created for this tag is the perfect accent for a wedding project, or for any romantic project. It softens the patterns and colors of the patterned papers and helps draw your eye to the "Best Wishes" sentiment. Personalizing this tag makes it not only perfect to adorn the bride and groom's gift, but also a treasured keepsake for years to come. Try using an engagement photo of the bride and groom as I did (my daughter Terri and son-in-law Laren are featured here) to make this tag even more special.

Supplies: alpha stickers, patterned paper, paint (Making Memories); embroidery floss (DMC); glitter glue (Ranger); pearl pins (Maya Road); self-adhesive pearls (The Paper Studio); rhinestones (Darice); faceted embellishments, grungepaper (Tim Holtz); punches (Whale of a Punch); glitter, punches (EK Success); decoupage medium (iLoveToCreate); chandelier bead (Laura's Vintage Garden); other: seam binding, vintage buttons, baker's twine

What You'll Need

patterned paper, paper trimmer, scallop-edge paper punch

1 Cut a strip of patterned paper that is 1½" (4cm) wide. The strip should be a bit longer than the desired length of your project (you'll cut the trim to fit once it is complete).

2 Place the paper into the punch, lining up the end of the paper with the center mark of the punch. Punch the paper.

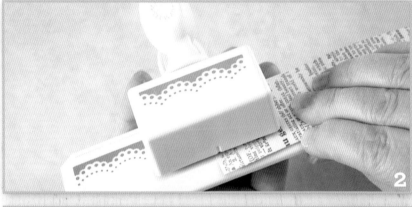

3 After you punch the paper, slide the paper to the left inside the punch. Line up the punched portion with the guide on the punch. Punch the next section of paper. Repeat this step until the paper is punched from one end to the other.

4 Rotate the strip and place the unpunched side of the patterned paper in the punch. Very carefully align the paper in the punch so that the scallops on each edge will match. Make the first punch, remove the paper from the punch and check to make sure the designs line up. Continue punching until the entire length is punched.

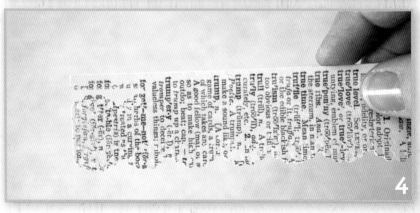

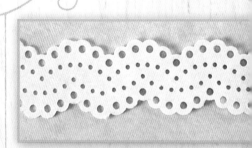

More Delightful Options

Instead of creating a trim where the scallops match, you can offset the scallops to create a trim that looks like rickrack. This small change gives this technique a whole new look!

Embellished Chipboard Frame

This photo of me and my brother is one of my favorites. I still remember what we were doing when the photo was taken—I was picking flowers and he was looking at bugs. In spite of my love for this photo, I felt it needed some altering. The white space on this photo was too distracting, so I decided to frame the area I wanted to highlight. Customizing the frame with paint and ink helped it meld with the rest of the layout. To mask the background of the photo even more, I attached the title of the layout on top of the photo. These easy changes helped bring the photo into focus.

Supplies: patterned paper, alphabet stickers (October Afternoon); paint (Making Memories, Jenni Bowlin); ink (Clearsnap); glitter glue, ink, ultra thick embossing enamel (Ranger); stamp (Studio 490 by Wendy Vecchi); glitter, chipboard letters, chipboard numbers, chipboard frame, doily transparencies (Maya Road); punch (EK Success); fine silver German glass glitter (German Corner LLC); staple (Tim Holtz); other: seam binding, baker's twine

What You'll Need

chipboard frame, acrylic paint, paintbrush, ink, stamp, acrylic block, embossing medium, ultra thick embossing enamel (UTEE), glitter, nonstick craft mat, heat tool, glitter glue

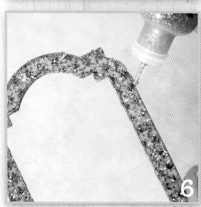

1 Using a paintbrush, paint a chipboard frame with acrylic paint. Let the paint dry.

2 Lightly ink the painted area with creamy brown ink.

3 Attach a stamp to an acrylic block. Apply ink to the stamp and stamp the painted chipboard frame.

4 Apply embossing medium to the painted and stamped side of the chipboard frame.

5 Place the chipboard frame onto a nonstick craft mat and pour UTEE (I used clear UTEE) over the chipboard frame. Tap off any excess. Use a heat tool to melt the UTEE. Once the UTEE has completely melted, sprinkle a small amount of glitter on top of the UTEE (I used fine glass glitter). If the UTEE hardens before you apply the glitter, just reheat the UTEE as needed.

6 Accent the inner and outer edges of the chipboard frame using glitter glue.

Altered Acrylic Embellishment

When I was growing up, my aunt always seemed like such a jet-setter to me. My uncle, her husband, was a pilot, so they got to go to many wonderful places all over the world. She also went to many conventions, and she says the convention she was going to in this photo, at age fifteen, started it all. I just love my aunt's outfit in this picture, and I mimicked her look with a cream and red color scheme in this layout. Altering the acrylic embellishments and metal flowers with Copic markers added perfect pops of red to the layout while the floral patterned paper perfectly accented the floral pattern on her dress. Accenting some of the zigzag stitching around the layout with red embroidery floss helps pull all the embellishments on this layout together.

Supplies: patterned paper (3ndypapir.no, The Girls' Paperie); doily (Wilton); glitter glue, gloss medium (Ranger); metal flowers (Making Memories); embroidery floss (DMC); flower stick pins, star stick pin, ink, acrylic houses, spray ink (Maya Road); flocked flowers (Vintage Street Market); punch, decorative scissors (Fiskars); chipboard letters (Advantus); ink (Clearsnap); German glass glitter (German Corner LLC); glitter, micro beads (Art-C Mixed Media); self-adhesive pearls (The Paper Studio); other: Copic markers, baker's twine, vintage buttons, book page, vintage ledger paper

What You'll Need

acrylic embellishment, Copic marker, gloss medium, glitter, micro beads, glitter glue, flower embellishment, strong liquid adhesive

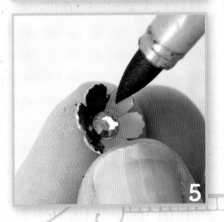

1 Using a Copic marker, color one side of the acrylic embellishment.

2 Apply gloss medium to of the acrylic embellishment, on top of the Copic marker coloring.

3 Lightly sprinkle glitter over the gloss medium, then micro beads on top of the glitter. Let the gloss medium dry.

4 Accent the edges of the embellishment using glitter glue.

5 Color the flower with a Copic marker to match the acrylic embellishment.

6 Using a strong liquid adhesive, attach the flower to the house.

More Project Details

I often join elements in my projects by sewing them together using a sewing machine. On this piece, I used zigzag stitching in several places. This is a nice touch to add to a project, but a subtle one. To make this detail pack more of a punch, I sometimes sew over the machine stitches with embroidery floss. To try this on a project of your own, simply thread a sewing needle with one strand of embroidery floss and randomly stitch over the machine-stitched zigzag.

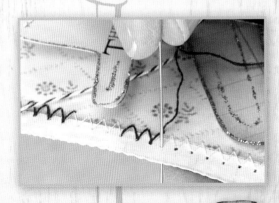

Chipboard Cameo

Even though this card is designed to celebrate a wedding, it could easily be used for any holiday or special occasion with a few simple changes. Instead of using the romantic cameo shown here, accent the center of the card with an embellishment more appropriate for the occasion you're celebrating. Try other chipboard shapes, altered chipboard embellishments or even buttons. I'm sure you will come up with so many fun ways to use this card.

Supplies: patterned paper (The Girls' Paperie, Anna Griffin Inc.); rub-ons (Jenni Bowlin); cameo, ink, mini chipboard tag, rose organza trim (Maya Road); gloss medium, paint, ink, glitter glue (Ranger); self-adhesive pearls (The Paper Studio); other: book page

What You'll Need

ornate chipboard embellishment, acrylic paint, paintbrush, ink, chipboard oval, patterned paper, glue stick, craft knife, cutting mat, sanding block, chipboard silhouette, liquid adhesive, gloss medium, chipboard flower, self-adhesive pearls, glitter glue, seam binding, scissors, fabric adhesive

1 Paint the ornate chipboard piece and let the paint dry completely.

2 Ink the ornate chipboard piece with creamy brown ink.

3 Apply a glue stick adhesive to the chipboard oval and place the oval glue side down on patterned paper. Use a craft knife to trim around the edge of the chipboard piece.

4 Sand the edges of the chipboard oval. Ink the edges of the piece as well.

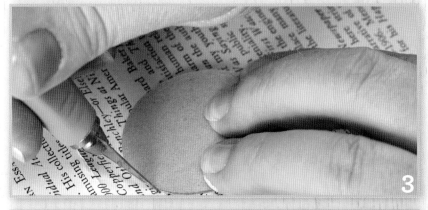

5 Paint the chipboard silhouette. Allow the paint to dry completely.

6 Use a liquid adhesive to attach the chipboard oval on top of the ornate chipboard piece. Adhere the chipboard silhouette to the chipboard oval.

7 Apply gloss medium to the exposed edges of the ornate chipboard piece.

8 Using white ink, ink the entire chipboard flower, then ink the edges of the flower using light brown ink.

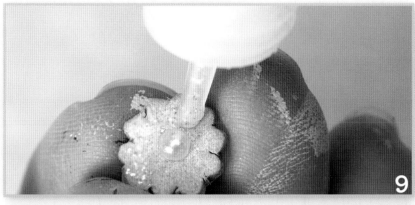

9 Accent the center of the chipboard flower with a self-adhesive pearl. Apply glitter glue to the chipboard flower. Allow the glue to dry completely.

10 Use a liquid adhesive to attach the flower to the silhouette. Create a necklace on the silhouette using 3 self-adhesive pearls.

11 Accent the edges of the ornate chipboard piece and the chipboard oval with glitter glue.

12 Cut a 6" (15cm) length of seam binding, fold it in half and snip the ends on a diagonal. Use fabric adhesive to attach the seam binding to the back of the cameo.

More Delightful Options

If white is not the color choice for you, you can easily tint the seam binding and white organza rose trim using Maya Mist or another spray ink. Tinting or dyeing your trims allows you to color coordinate them for any of your projects.

Paper Party Hat

You can customize this fun and festive hat in so many ways. The hat begins with patterned paper, and your selection will influence the look of the entire project, so choose carefully! You can also create different looks at the brim of the hat with the paper punch and trim you use. Try using the *Tissue Paper Trim* from page 16 on this hat instead of marabou. Finally, add a decorative element to the top of the hat—it's like the cherry on the sundae. If a crepe paper rosette doesn't suit your taste, how about a large pom-pom? Make this hat your own!

Supplies: patterned paper (Anna Griffin Inc.); chipboard number (Heidi Swapp); ink (Clearsnap); crepe paper (Designware); glitter glue, gloss medium (Ranger); tiny alphas (Making Memories); punches, glitter (EK Success); decorative scissors (Fiskars); self-adhesive pearl (Mark Richards); decoupage medium (iLoveToCreate); marabou (Zucker Feather Products); other: seam binding

What You'll Need

patterned paper, paper trimmer, scallop-edge paper punch, bone folder, scissors, decoupage medium, paintbrush, glitter, glitter glue, marabou trim, strong liquid adhesive

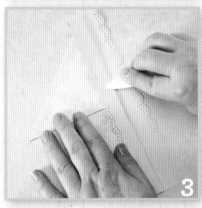

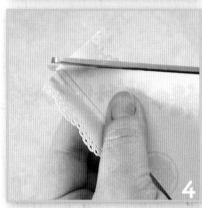

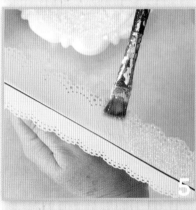

1 Cut a piece of patterned paper to 8½" × 11" (22cm × 28cm) with a paper trimmer. Using a scallop-edge paper punch, punch both short edges of the patterned paper. Fold the paper in half so that the punched edges match up. Use a bone folder to create a crisp fold.

2 With the folded edge at the top, fold the right corner down toward the center of the punched edge. Fold the left corner down toward the center of the punched edge as well, so that the folded edges meet in the center. Use a bone folder on both folded edges.

3 Fold the top punched edge upward over the folded edges. Smooth the fold with a bone folder.

4 Use scissors to snip the square ends of the punched border to make the ends flush with the folded edges.

5 Repeat steps 3 and 4 to fold and trim the other punched edge. Apply decoupage medium to the punched borders with a paintbrush. Sprinkle glitter onto the wet decoupage medium, tap off any excess and let the medium dry.

6 Accent the scallops on the punched border with glitter glue. Allow the glitter glue to dry.

7 Fold the corners of the hat inward toward each other to open up the hat.

8 Accent the bottom edge of the hat with white marabou trim applied with a strong liquid adhesive.

Crepe Paper Doll

These sweet dolls would be the perfect gift to give to each of your bridesmaids as a keepsake for being in your wedding party. Each doll could be personalized to match its recipient with easy changes to hair color and skin tone. They would also make lovely place cards at a bridal shower—just prop a name card against the doll's skirt. And how cute would these paper dolls look on a table setting for a little girls' tea party? They'd brighten the table and would be a perfect party favor. With a few minor alterations, these crepe paper dolls could even be turned into angel tree toppers or centerpieces for the Christmas season.

Supplies: crepe paper (Melissa Frances); embroidery floss (DMC); wooden bead (Crafts, Etc!); paint (FolkArt, Ranger); crystal chandelier bead (Maya Road); decorative scissors (Fiskars); rhinestones (Advantus); chenille bump stem, miniature flocked flowers (Laura's Vintage Garden); other: seam binding, tulle, baker's twine

What You'll Need

chenille bump stem, crepe paper, scissors, sewing needle, thread, liquid adhesive, pinking shears, seam binding, flocked flowers, wooden bead, acrylic paint, paintbrush, permanent marker, tulle, fabric adhesive

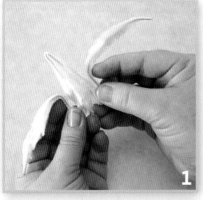

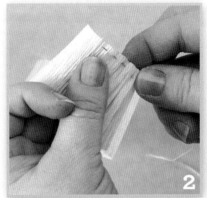

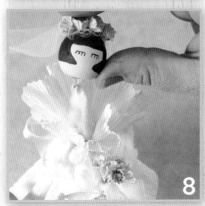

1 Bend a chenille bump stem in half (forming the neck). Bend each end upward to form the waist, and bend stems outward to form the arms.

2 Cut 2 pieces of crepe paper: 4" × 12" (10cm × 30cm) and 2" × 12" (5cm × 30cm). Stitch along the top edge of the larger piece of crepe paper to form a skirt. Gather the stitches and secure the thread ends with a knot to form a cone. Repeat on the smaller piece of crepe paper to form the dress top.

3 Place the chenille stem into the small crepe paper cone. Snip the sides of the crepe paper, sliding the arms into the top of the dress. Attach the edges of the snipped sections above the arms with a bit of liquid adhesive.

4 Trim the top edge of the crepe paper with pinking shears.

5 Apply liquid adhesive to the gathered portion of the skirt and attach it to the chenille stem. Tie a piece of seam binding around the waist of the doll and secure it with a bow.

6 Tie a piece of seam binding around a small bunch of flocked flowers. Secure the flowers in the hands of the doll by bending the chenille stem around the bouquet.

7 Paint a wooden bead with flesh-colored paint. Paint the doll's hair and draw the eyes on using a permanent marker. For a bride doll, attach tulle to the doll's head using fabric adhesive. Accent the veil to match the doll's bouquet. For a bridesmaid, accent with a single flower.

8 Push the wooden bead onto the chenille stem neck. Secure the bead with adhesive.

Felt Gift Bow

This felt gift bow can be used in a variety of ways, but I decided to make mine the centerpiece of a bridal brooch inspired by a homecoming mum. In Texas, mums are nearly as important to homecoming as football! And the bigger, the better is how it goes with these things. Just because you're out of high school doesn't mean you can't join in on the fun, too. This would be perfect for a bride-to-be to wear at a wedding shower or a rehearsal dinner. I thought it would be fun to create one with a simple, old-fashioned feel, so I chose felt, vintage laces and trims, but you can create these out of any materials you like. I think one made of burlap would be gorgeous, especially with streamers made of linen and muslin. There is no right or wrong way when it comes to making mums.

Supplies: satin edge trim (Maya Road), felt (CPE), vintage lace (Laura's Vintage Garden); other: burlap, vintage sheet music, vintage milk bottle cap, vintage button

What You'll Need

felt, paper trimmer, permanent marker, fabric adhesive, small embellishments (optional)

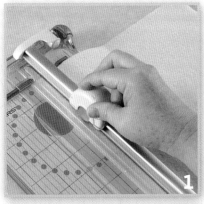

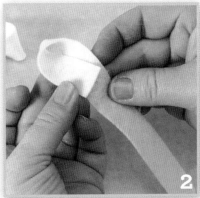

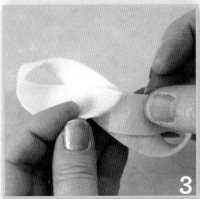

1 Using a paper trimmer, cut 3 felt strips, each ¾" × 8½" (2cm × 22cm). Cut 3 more strips, each ¾" × 7" (2cm × 18cm).

2 Make a small mark at the center of each strip with a permanent marker. Place a small amount of fabric adhesive on the mark. Grasp one end and fold it toward the mark, twisting it once. Secure the end in the fabric adhesive.

3 Repeat step 2 to secure the other end of the strip. Allow the fabric adhesive to dry.

4 Repeat steps 2 and 3 with all felt strips. Place a small amount of fabric adhesive on the center of one of the larger folded felt pieces. Place a second larger felt piece on top of the adhesive, forming an X. Add a small amount of fabric adhesive to the center of the top felt piece. Place the last larger felt piece on top of the stack, spacing it between the other 2.

5 Repeat step 4 to add all 3 smaller felt pieces to the stack. Arrange the felt pieces so the tips of the smaller pieces line up between the larger pieces.

6 Place an embellishment in the center of the bow. Here, I added a chipboard piece covered in vintage sheet music topped with a vintage rhinestone button. If you'd prefer, you can also finish the bow with a piece of felt in the center. Cut 1 piece of felt to ¾" × 3" (2cm × 8cm). Use fabric adhesive to join this piece to form a loop, then glue the loop at the center of the bow.

More Delightful Options

This mum would be a great topper for a baby shower gift in either a pink or blue color scheme.

Lisa & Richard 1966

chapter four

Autumn

In southeast Texas, we don't have many trees that change colors in autumn. To give us a taste of the season, each year my grandmother would send maple leaves from her yard that were the most gorgeous shades of yellow, orange and red. Gram would iron them between two sheets of wax paper, and I would tape them to my bedroom window—the leaves made it look as though I had stained glass windows. I reflect on this simple, loving gesture each autumn. My family had other autumnal traditions as well; my mom and I would make caramel apples while we planned Halloween decorations and costumes. On Thanksgiving, my brother, sister and I would wake up to the smell of a turkey cooking, excited to watch the Thanksgiving Day parades. Autumn is full of special celebrations!

In this chapter, I will show you how to create projects that celebrate all autumn has to offer. I'll show you how to turn a stack of punched paper into a Halloween pumpkin on page 106. We'll also create projects for every generation in your family—the project on page 100 celebrates new arrivals, while those on pages 108 and 112 honor grandparents. If you need a creative boost, soak in autumn's inspiration with all your senses—I know the scents of fall inspire me in so many different ways. Whether it's the smell of pumpkin pies baking or hot apple cider with cinnamon sticks simmering on the stove, these scents make me think of all the gorgeous colors and special moments autumn brings. Inspiration comes in so many different ways and is always around if you just take a moment to let it all in.

Altered Bottle Brush Tree

The fun thing about creating these trees is that the sky is the limit! You can dye them any color to match any holiday or special occasion. To take the look even further, use a paintbrush to apply a thin layer of adhesive, then roll the tree in a pile of mica or glitter. Once you tap off the excess you'll have a shimmery tree that is ready to decorate any project. These trees are perfect for shadow boxes, and if you trim the back of a tree to make it flat, it is a great embellishment for a card or tag. Go wild with this technique!

Supplies: spray ink, bottle caps, star stick pins, jewel pins (Maya Road); wooden candlestick (Crafts, Etc!); wooden spools, wooden circle, wooden fence (Darice); acrylic paint, buttons, calendar flag banner (Jenni Bowlin); glitter glue (Ranger); flocked flower (Vintage Street Market); rhinestones (Advantus); punch (Fiskars); ink (Clearsnap); chalkboard paint (Krylon); self-adhesive pearls (Michaels); other: bottle brush trees, seam binding, vintage glass beads, book page, Copic marker

What You'll Need

bottle brush tree, bleach, water, bowl, paper towels, nonstick craft mat, ink spray (two colors)

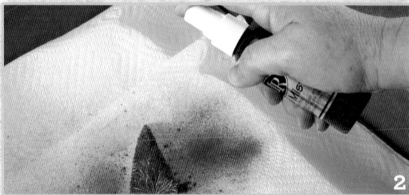

1 Mix 3 parts water and 1 part bleach into a bowl. Place a bottle brush tree into the mixture and let it soak until it turns off-white. Remove the tree from the mixture and rinse it well with cold water. Pat the tree dry with a paper towel, then allow it to dry completely.

2 For a tree that is one color, use ink spray directly on the tree. Work over paper towels or newspaper in a cardboard box.

3 For a tree with multiple colors, mix water and ink spray together in a bowl or cup. Dip the tree approximately two-thirds of the way into the mixture.

4 Let the tree dry completely. If you dip the tree again before it is completely dry, the new color will bleed up the tree, so be patient! Mix water with a second color of ink spray and dip the tree approximately one-third of the way into the mixture. Allow the tree to dry completely again. If you like, accent the tree with beads, glitter, or anything else that strikes your fancy.

More Project Details

The large bottle cap base of this sculpture has been painted with chalkboard paint so a Halloween sentiment can be added with chalk and changed easily.

Gesso and Dye Based Mist Paint

I created this layout in honor of my grandparents; both of them have passed away, but I wanted to celebrate them and the family they created. I started by creating a background for the layout that resembled a patchwork quilt—a symbol that reminds me of family. I customized the colors for the quilt by mixing gesso and dye mist together. Mixing gesso and dye mist is a great way to customize paint colors. You can create several shades of the same color depending on the amount of mist you add to the gesso. The more mist you add, the darker the color, and the less mist you add, the lighter the color. Just make sure you mix enough of the paint color you will be using, because trying to recreate the same color again will be difficult. Trust me on this one.

Supplies: patterned paper (3ndypapir.no); gesso, spray ink, chipboard frames, chipboard alphas, chipboard numbers (Maya Road); texture plates (Sizzix); leaf die (Cuttlebug); watercolor paper, micro beads (C-Thru Ruler Company); glitter glue, ink, ultra thick embossing enamel, gloss medium (Ranger); ink (Clearsnap); decorative scissors (Fiskars); self-adhesive pearls (The Paper Studio); jewelers tags (American Tag Co.); tiny alphas, paint (Making Memories); embroidery floss (DMC); other: seam binding, eyelets

What You'll Need

gesso, ink spray, paintbrush, nonstick craft mat, cardstock, ink, glitter glue

1 Apply a small amount of gesso onto a non-stick craft mat. Add ink spray to the gesso. The more ink you add, the darker the color will be. Mix enough gesso and ink to complete your project—trying to get the exact color you just mixed later is not easy to repeat.

2 Use the mixed gesso and ink as you would any paint. For this project, I painted textured cardstock with my mixture.

3 Allow the paint to dry completely. To mute the color, apply a light brown ink on top of the paint.

4 If desired, embellish the painted surface with glitter glue.

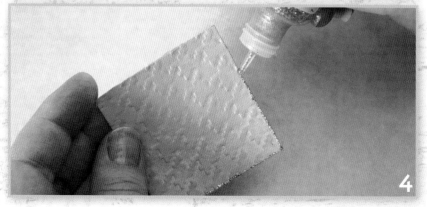

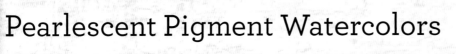

Pearlescent Pigment Watercolors

This photo of my brother and me is one of my favorites. As you can guess from the huge smile on my face, I was quite excited to be holding him. He was an October baby, so for this layout I decided to go with a color scheme that is nontraditional for a baby item. Instead of using the expected pink or blue, I went with the warm tones of autumn to celebrate an autumn baby. The pearlescent pigments give a subtle touch of color to the cabinet card frame, complementing the color scheme I chose. This cabinet card was originally part of a mini album, but I disguised the holes in the cabinet card by threading seam binding through them and accenting the bow with flocked flowers and baubles. Never be afraid to repurpose an embellishment to suit your own needs—creativity can yield beautiful results!

Lisa & Richard 1966

Supplies: patterned paper (The Girls' Paperie); glitter glue, pearlescent pigment powder, pearlescent pigment spray (Ranger); cabinet card, pearl charm (Jenni Bowlin); gold leafing pen (Krylon); decorative scissors (Fiskars); self-adhesive pearls (Michaels); bauble charm (Tim Holtz); vintage lace (Laura's Vintage Garden); other: seam binding, vintage buttons, vintage ledger paper, flocked flowers, baker's twine

What You'll Need

pearlescent pigment powder, pearlescent pigment spray, paintbrush, nonstick craft mat, paper towel, cardstock, glitter glue

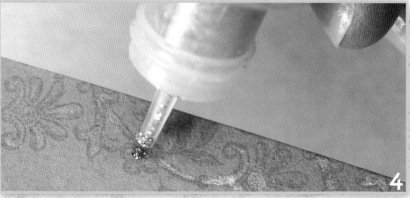

1 Apply a few squirts of pearlescent pigment spray to a nonstick craft mat. Use the end of your paintbrush to scoop a small amount of pearlescent pigment powder in a matching color onto the liquid. Mix the two together with the handle end of the paintbrush.

2 Dip the brush end of the paintbrush lightly into the mixture. Before you begin to paint, make sure your paintbrush is not too wet; if it is, dab the brush on a paper towel to remove the excess liquid. If your paintbrush is too wet, the color could bleed onto the frame.

3 Begin painting on the frame. The piece I painted was a cabinet card from a mini album set that had a floral pattern stamped on it. I painted over that pattern using a very fine brush.

4 Allow the project to dry completely. Accent the pattern you painted with glitter glue if you desire.

More Project Details

The ledger paper you see in this layout was not meant to be stitched, but I accidentally cut the ledger paper to the wrong measurements. I did not want to waste this paper, so I decided to sew it back together with a zigzag stitch, and now it looks like it was supposed to be that way. (But now you know the truth.) Sometimes what you think is a mistake really turns out perfectly OK.

Molded Ultra Thick Embossing Enamel

Using silicone molds with melted ultra thick embossing enamel is a simple way to create unique embellishments for your projects. I like to look for silicone ice cube trays, candy molds and cupcake baking molds. You can find lots of different molds in cake- and candy-making supplies. During the holidays, check the dollar section of stores—I have found many cute seasonal molds at a great price this way.

Supplies: ultra thick embossing enamel, alcohol ink, ink, glitter glue, pearlescent pigment powder, pearlescent pigment spray (Ranger); florist tape, florist wire (Fiskars); modeling film, stamp (Studio 490 by Wendy Vecchi); patterned paper (Jenni Bowlin); die (Sizzix); leaves (Laura's Vintage Garden); doily (Wilton); other: book page, seam binding

What You'll Need

floral wire, wire cutters, pliers, ultra thick embossing enamel (UTEE) (two colors), melting pot, silicone mold, embossing medium pen, heat tool

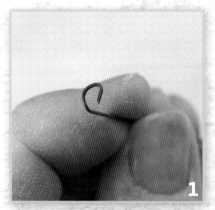

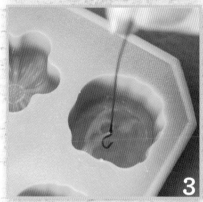

1 Cut a piece of floral wire to the length you desire for your flower stem. Use a pair of pliers to bend the end into a small loop.

2 Pour UTEE into a melting pot and follow the manufacturer's instructions to melt the UTEE. Once the UTEE is completely melted, carefully pour it into the silicone mold. My mold was deeper than I wanted my flower to be, so I only partially filled the mold.

3 While the UTEE is still melted, quickly place the bent end of the wire into the UTEE. Hold the wire so that the loop is about halfway through the thickness of the UTEE. Hold the wire in place until the UTEE sets.

4 Once the UTEE has set completely, remove the flower from the mold. Use an embossing medium pen on the raised areas of the flower. Dip the flower into a second color of UTEE. Tap off any excess, then carefully heat the new color of UTEE. Do not hold the heat tool in one place too long or it will distort the shape of your flower.

More Delightful Options

It's easy to make your own mold to create unique UTEE embellishments. Start by finding an object you'd like to replicate. Mix two-part molding putty, then form it into a ball. Press the object you've chosen into the putty, applying even pressure. Allow the putty to completely cure. Once it has hardened, remove the object from the putty. You can now use this mold to create unique embellishments for your projects.

Pleated Ribbon Rose

Placing a centerpiece on a side table or buffet is one way I like to decorate for the holidays, and this adorable hat will be used as a centerpiece for many Halloweens to come! I didn't want a traditional pom-pom topping, so I decided to use a pleated ribbon rose at the top of the hat. The addition of a memo pin allows me to place vintage images, Halloween greetings or even an invitation on top. After placing the pleated ribbon rose on top of the hat, I decided to attach the same roses around the base of the hat to help frame the pumpkin images. I think having the added black trim gives it even more of a festive feel.

Supplies: patterned paper, lace (The Girls' Paperie); satin pleat trim, velvet trim (Maya Road); creative scraps (Crafty Secrets Heartwarming Vintage); pens (Advantus); ink (Clearsnap); decorative scissors (Fiskars); pumpkin die cuts (Target); glitter glue (Ranger); pearls (Mark Richards)

What You'll Need
satin pleat trim, scissors, fabric adhesive

1 Cut a piece of satin pleated ribbon to approximately 12" (30cm).

2 Pinch the end of the trim between your thumb and forefinger. Begin to roll the trim around your finger.

3 Continue rolling the trim until you get to the opposite end. Secure the end of the trim to the rose with a dot of fabric adhesive. Remove the rose from your finger and apply a thin coating of fabric adhesive to the bottom of the rose to further secure the fabric to itself and to the hat.

More Project Details

The pumpkin embellishments on this hat were once part of an invitation to a Halloween party. I thought they'd add the perfect touch to this project, so I cut them out of the invitation using a craft knife and attached them to the hat using foam squares.

I was so excited when I found these invitations in the clearance section after Halloween—I just loved the vintage feel of the pumpkins and knew I could use them several different ways. After each holiday season, shop the clearance aisle to see if you can find items to turn into embellishments.

Paper Baby Shoe

This project would make a beautiful centerpiece for a baby shower and later a pretty decoration for a nursery. At the shower, if the new parents-to-be know the sex of their baby, you can place pink or blue bows on top; if they don't know yet, a color such as yellow or green will work perfectly. You can also turn these shoes into baby shower favors—make the shoes, then fill them with small candies. Wrap them in tulle, tie them with a pink or blue bow, and you're done!

Supplies: kraft paper (The Paper Studio); patterned paper (My Mind's Eye); paint, ink (Jenni Bowlin); ink (Clearsnap); decoupage medium (iLoveToCreate); felt (CPE); glitter glue (Ranger); scallop base, chipboard alphabet, chipboard numbers (Maya Road); decorative scissors (Fiskars); other: papier mâché blocks, vintage sheet music, seam binding

What You'll Need

templates (see page 103), copier, cardstock, pencil, scissors, patterned paper, glue stick, ink, glitter glue, seam binding, felt, fabric adhesive, scallop scissors

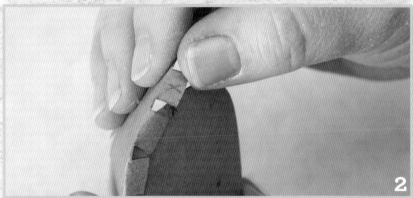

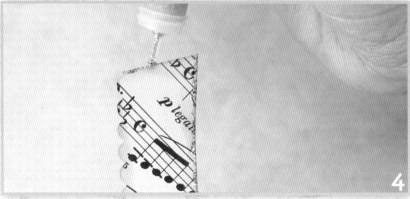

1 Make a copy of the templates on page 103, then cut the templates out. Lay templates 1, 2 and 3 on the cardstock and trace them. Lay templates 3 and 4 on the patterned paper and trace them. Cut out each of the pieces.

2 Fold the tabs in on Piece 1 and glue the tabs to Piece 2. Align the marks on the pieces as you go.

3 Apply light brown ink to the edges of the patterned paper pieces.

4 Embellish the edges of the patterned paper pieces with glitter glue.

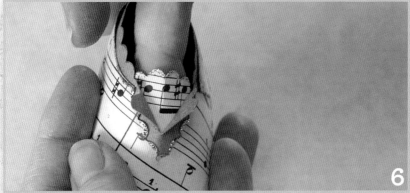

5 Using a glue stick, attach Piece 4 to Piece 1.

6 Glue the patterned paper version of Piece 3 on top of the cardstock version of Piece 3. Trim along the dotted line on Piece 1 and fold back the tabs. Glue the combined Piece 3 behind the opening.

7 Create a bow using seam binding. Attach it to the shoe with fabric adhesive. Apply fabric adhesive to the bottom of the shoe and attach it to a piece of felt. Cut around the shoe using scallop scissors.

8 Embellish the top and bottom edges of the shoe with glitter glue.

More Delightful Options

After the birth of their baby, the new parents can add their baby's name, birth date, weight and length to the side of a block to complete the cherished keepsake.

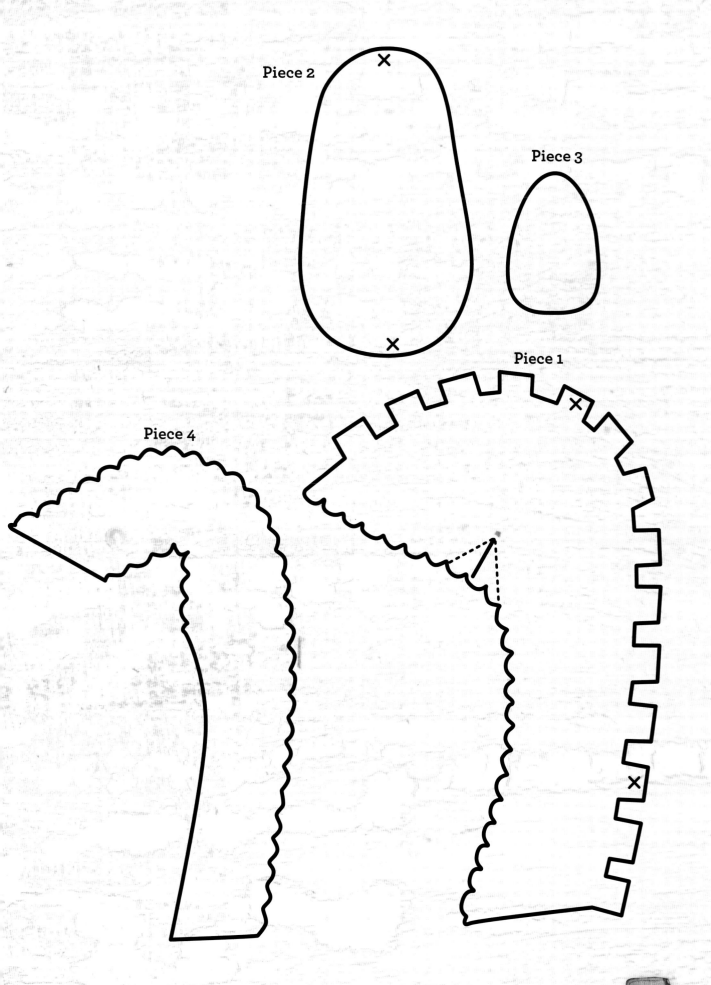

Piece 2

Piece 3

Piece 1

Piece 4

Altered Die Cut

I created this tag to be displayed in a floral arrangement during Thanksgiving. I packed it with elements that remind me of fall, including burlap, felt and plaid along with hues of yellow, orange and red. I arranged the altered die-cut leaves so that they would look as though they were falling from the tree—this is how my grandmother would iron the autumn leaves she sent to me. The altered chandelier bead at the bottom of the tag is tinted using a Copic marker, then stamped with archival ink and a plaid stamp. I think it is the perfect embellishment to top off this tag.

Supplies: watercolor paper, beads (C-Thru Ruler Company Art-C Collection); pearlescent pigment spray, gloss medium, ultra thick embossing enamel, tag, glitter glue, ink (Ranger); chipboard letters (Maya Road); felt (CPE); stamp (Studio 490 by Wendy Vecchi); dies (Provo Craft); other: sheet music, baker's twine, Copic markers

What You'll Need

watercolor paper, leaf die, Distress inks (two colors), blending tool, embossing medium pen, ultra thick embossing enamel (UTEE), tweezers, heat tool, glitter glue

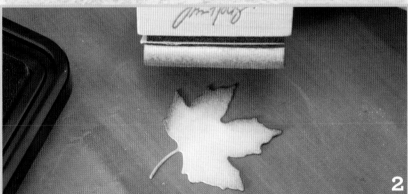

1 Using a die-cut machine, cut a leaf out of watercolor paper. Apply your lighter colored ink (yellow or orange) to a blending tool and ink the entire leaf.

2 Apply your darker ink (orange if yellow was used in step 1; red if orange was used) to the blending tool and apply the ink to the edges of the leaf.

3 Use an embossing medium pen on the edges of the leaf. If you'd like some detailing inside the leaf, apply embossing medium there as well. Holding the maple leaf with tweezers, dip the leaf into gold UTEE, then tap off the excess UTEE. Melt the UTEE with a heat tool.

4 Embellish the leaf with glitter glue for extra sparkle.

3-D Paper Embellishment

Halloween is such a fun time for people both young and old. The main attractions of this Halloween card are the paper embellishments—so much easier to make than they look. Create them using a stack of identical die-cut shapes stitched together, and of course, embellished. I also embellished the polka dot patterns on the paper as well as the witches hair, hat and broom with glitter glue. Lastly, I topped off the tag with a black seam binding bow. These little accents pull the entire card together for a truly festive Halloween feel.

Supplies: patterned paper (Graphic 45); blank card (DCWV); ink (Clearsnap); chipboard wings, ink (Maya Road); glitter (Making Memories); gloss medium, glitter glue (Ranger); punches, decorative scissors (Fiskars); chenille stem (Laura's Vintage Garden); other: baker's twine, seam binding

What You'll Need

patterned paper, large scallop circle punch, sewing machine and thread, glitter glue (two colors), leaf punch, brown chenille stem, wire cutters, strong liquid adhesive, tweezers

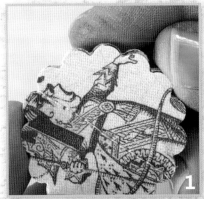

1 Using a large, scallop circle punch, punch 5 circles out of patterned paper. Stack the circles on top of each other and, using a sewing machine, sew a straight stitch down the center of the stacked circles.

2 Bend the stack of circles in half along the stitched line.

3 Fan the stack out so that the papers form a rounded shape.

4 Accent each piece of paper with glitter glue. (I used Distress Stickles in Spiced Marmalade and Stickles in Diamond.)

5 Using a small leaf punch, punch 3 leaves out of patterned paper. I did not have a leaf punch small enough to suit my taste, so I used only the leaf part of an apple punch I had on hand.

6 Using wire cutters, cut a small piece of brown chenille stem to create the stem for the pumpkin. Attach the stem and leaves to the top of the pumpkin using a strong liquid adhesive and tweezers.

Fabric Cuff

Grandmothers seem to have everything they need or want, so finding a gift for Grandparent's Day can be quite the challenge. This fabric cuff would be a wonderful handmade gift for just this very occasion. Grandmothers love any and all things you create just for them. You can use a wide variety of trims and fabric when making these cuffs. When purchasing fabric and trims for your cuff, check the remnant section of fabric stores—you can purchase high-end fabrics there at a low cost. You can also use fabric from dishtowels, washcloths and other thrift store finds to make the base and flowers for your cuffs.

Supplies: felt (CPE); satin pleat trim, rose organza trim (Maya Road); vintage lace, vintage leaves (Laura's Vintage Garden); self-adhesive pearls (The Paper Studio); other: doily, burlap, vintage button, toilet paper roll

What You'll Need

cardboard tube, scissors, lace, fabric adhesive, burlap, felt, scallop scissors, crocheted doily, satin pleat trim, self-adhesive pearl, silk leaves, silk flowers, buttons

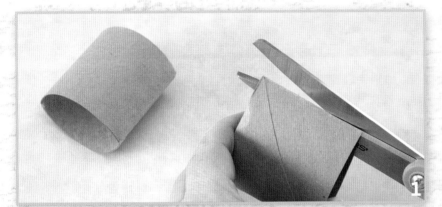

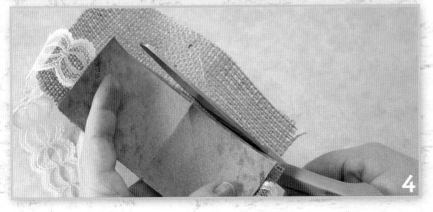

1 Cut 2 pieces of cardboard tube to the height you desire for your cuff. I find that cutting a roll of toilet paper in half gives me the perfect size. Flatten both pieces to form 2 creases on each tube. Cut along 1 crease on each tube.

2 Cut 2 pieces of lace, each 12" (30cm) in length (these will serve as ties; I like my ties long, so 12" [30cm] works for me, but you can trim yours shorter if you like). Using a fabric adhesive, attach a piece of lace to each end of one of the cardboard pieces.

3 Glue the second piece of cardboard on top of the first, sandwiching the lace.

4 Cut a piece of burlap to fit the cardboard exactly. Set this piece aside for now.

5 Cut 2 pieces of felt that are each approximately ½" (13mm) wider and longer than the cardboard. Using fabric adhesive, attach 1 piece of felt to the top piece of cardboard and 1 to the bottom piece.

6 Using scallop scissors, trim the top and bottom edge of the felt. Use fabric adhesive to attach the burlap piece to the top felt piece; center it between the top and bottom felt scallops.

7 Cut a crocheted doily in half. Attach both pieces to the burlap piece using fabric adhesive, lining up the cut edges of the doily with the outer edges of the burlap.

8 Cut a piece of satin pleat trim to 12" (30cm). Apply fabric adhesive to the back of a large button and attach the trim to the back of the button. Wrap the trim around the button to form a flower. Secure the end of the trim to the flower with a dot of fabric adhesive.

9 Glue the satin flower to the center of the cuff. Accent the center of the flower with a self-adhesive pearl.

10 Glue 2 silk leaves to one side of the flower and 1 silk leaf to the other side.

11 Attach small silk flowers to the cuff on either side of the central flower.

12 Accent the cuff with matching buttons.

Paper Rose

I have always admired my grandparents—each one held a special place in my heart. I wanted this card to show some of those feelings, so I festooned it with lovely handmade roses. These roses have to be made with care, so they add a very special touch to a project. I also nestled the word "Admire" among the roses to convey my message of love. The pretty lace, buttons, and pearls I included add to the warm, pretty look of this card.

A BUTTERFLY'S HOME.

out in the sunshine
grasses grow tall,
among lilies
e winds bring;
soft air,
Admire oms
eing.

Supplies: patterned paper (Pink Paislee); punch (EK Success); ink (Clearsnap); vintage lace (Laura's Vintage Garden); transparency, chipboard flag banner, pearl charms (Jenni Bowlin); self-adhesive pearl (The Paper Studio); glitter glue (Ranger); embroidery floss (DMC); other: baker's twine, felt leaves, vintage buttons

What You'll Need

patterned paper, flower punch, ink, scissors, liquid adhesive, glitter glue

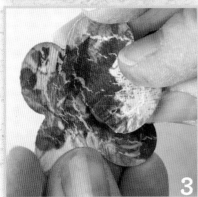

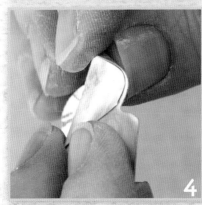

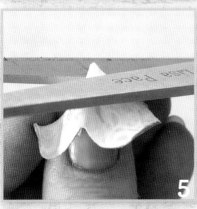

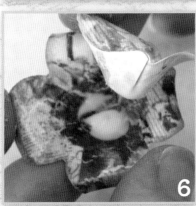

1 Punch 3 flowers out of patterned paper using a flower punch. Apply ink to the edges of all 3 flowers.

2 Cut between 2 petals to the center of the first flower (Flower 1). Cut the second flower into 2 pieces—one piece with 4 petals (Flower 2) and one piece with 1 petal (Flower 3). Cut the third flower into 2 pieces—one piece with 3 petals (Flower 4) and one piece with 2 petals (Flower 5).

3 On Flower 1, apply liquid adhesive to the top of the flower petal to the left of the cut. Place the petal to the right of the cut on top of the petal to the left of the cut. Hold the petals in place until the glue dries. Drawing the flower together in this way will give it somewhat of a cone shape and will make the piece dimensional. Curl the flower petals outward from the center.

4 Repeat step 3 on flowers 2 and 4. Roll Flower 5 (the piece with 2 petals) into a loose cone. Secure the cone with a bit of adhesive. Roll Flower 3 (the single petal) into a tight cone and secure it with liquid adhesive.

5 Trim the tips of flowers 2, 3, 4 and 5. This will help each layer nest well into the others.

6 Place liquid adhesive in the center of Flower 1; place Flower 2 inside Flower 1.

7 Repeat step 6 to place Flower 3 inside Flower 2, Flower 4 inside Flower 3, and finally Flower 5 inside Flower 4.

8 Embellish each petal with a bit of glitter glue.

More Seasonal Delights

I am thrilled that a gallery is included in this book so that I can showcase the versatility of the techniques featured in the previous chapters. All of the techniques in this book can be used in any season, but I picked some of my favorites and transform them here for you. I hope that seeing these techniques used in different ways and in different seasons will spark ideas for you. Don't be afraid to experiment, and remember: The only rules in art are the ones you make for yourself.

Autumn is one of my favorite seasons of the year. I love the crisp air, the changing leaves, and sitting on the couch with the fireplace going, wrapped up in a quilt. And the inspiration for this layout was just that—a quilt. To create the quilt-like base of this layout, I used patterned papers with warm tones pieced together with zigzag stitching. I accented three of the squares with felt maple leaves cut from a die. Instead of altering the leaves with ink and ultra thick embossing enamel, as I did with the *Altered Die Cut* on page 104, I used simple stitching and buttons. To incorporate more texture into the layout, I added burlap buttons. I also altered the crystal pins using Copic markers in orange and brown. And, of course, the edges of the cardstock and patterned papers are accented using glitter glue.

Supplies: patterned paper (Jenni Bowlin); felt (CPE); die (Provo Craft); chipboard buttons, crystal pins, tag (Maya Road); embroidery floss (DMC); glitter glue (Ranger); rub-ons (Melissa Frances); ink (Clearsnap); other: Copic markers, burlap, seam binding

I used two different techniques from previous projects here. First, I followed the steps for the *Decorative Pick* on page 70 to make the leaf picks on this warm, rich autumn project. I created the leaves using a leaf die and sandwiched a piece of wire between the leaves just as I did when creating the butterfly picks. I then bundled these picks into a bouquet. A cluster of clear chandelier beads twisted onto wire added just the right amount of shimmer and helped fill in the center area of the leaf bouquet without taking away from the simplicity of the leaves. The second technique I used was the *Scalloped Paper Fringe* on page 38—with a few changes. I only used a single layer of fringe on this tag, and instead of paper, I used felt. Also, to make it easier to keep each cut in the fringe the same length, I attached the scalloped felt to the back of the tag using fabric adhesive, then cut in between each scallop.

Supplies: patterned paper (Daisy D's); tag, glitter glue (Ranger); chandelier beads (Maya Road); wire (Darice); die (Sizzix); self-adhesive pearls (The Paper Studio); felt (CPE); other: book pages, seam binding

I love using cream-colored felt, and mixing it with burlap makes it even better. I think the roughness of burlap and the softness of felt make a wonderful textile combination. The burlap base of this wall hanging contrasts beautifully with the soft felt flowers that decorate it. The bottom two felt flowers on this wall hanging were created following the *Grungepaper Rose* technique from page 64. For these felt flowers, I skipped the paint and glitter glue, but adorned the flower centers using pearls. You could substitute buttons, rhinestones, stamens or beads at the center if you like. When you switch from grungepaper to felt to make these flowers, switch your adhesives as well. Use a fabric adhesive—if you don't, the felt will keep absorbing the adhesive and you will end up with a mess. Trust me on this one . . . I have experienced this firsthand!

Supplies: canvas dress, gingham trim, crochet trim, chipboard alphas (Maya Road); patterned paper, hanger (Crafty Secrets); pearls (The Paper Studio); felt (CPE); decorative scissors (Fiskars); tiny alphas (Making Memories); faceted bead (Tim Holtz); glitter glue (Ranger); other: vintage buttons, seam binding, embroidery floss, rosary beads

For this project, I painted the canvas and chipboard embellishments with custom colors I created using the *Gesso and Ink Paint* technique from page 92. I took this technique one step further by using glitter glue over the entire surface of each embellishment, instead of just the edges. Once the canvas piece was completely dry, I also enhanced it with machine stitching. I stitched two rows around the inside of the canvas square using cream thread and another two rows using an orange thread. I like the contrast this gives the canvas piece. You can use any of the techniques in this book as a starting point and add more to them as I did here.

Supplies: patterned paper, cardstock sticker (Sassafras Lass); canvas button, chipboard, spray ink (Maya Road); gesso, glitter glue (Ranger); ink (Clearsnap, Ranger); rub-ons (Melissa Frances)

The *Felt Gift Bow* from page 86 takes on a more traditional look in this winter card. To make this version, use the instructions from the summer chapter, but substitute patterned paper for felt. To scale down this bow, I cut six strips to $1/2$" × 6" (13mm × 15cm) and one strip to $1/2$" × $2^3/4$" (13mm × 7cm). I attached the small strip to the center of the bow instead of a button or other embellishment. For a more ornate look, try trimming the edges of each strip with decorative scissors before assembling the bow.

Supplies: patterned paper (The Girls' Paperie); ink (Clearsnap); glitter glue (Ranger); punch, lace doily (EK Success); rub-ons (Lily Bee Design); other: baker's twine

I used the *Paper Lace Trim* from page 72 to accent this new baby card. I thought this pretty embellishment was the perfect touch for this sweet card. To give the lace dimension, I attached it to the card using white foam squares. I also accented the paper lace with a strip of pink self-adhesive pearls. If you want custom pearls for your project, you can tint white or cream pearls using a Copic marker. Many objects can be tinted using Copic markers—this is an easy way to carry a color scheme throughout a project.

Supplies: patterned paper (The Girls' Paperie); vintage image (Crafty Secrets); crepe paper (Melissa Frances); glitter glue (Ranger); glitter, punch (EK Success); ink (Clearsnap); self-adhesive pearls (The Paper Studio, Mark Richards); heart pin, flower pin (Maya Road); other: seam binding

I wanted to break up all the red and green of the patterned papers in this layout so I decided to add a little unexpected pop of aqua. The *Altered Acrylic Embellishment* technique from page 76 was the perfect way to add this color. For this project, I colored the back of each acrylic snowflake using a Copic marker, but then instead of using gloss medium and dry glitter like I did in the summer chapter, I used glitter glue. If you are not a big fan of dry glitter, glitter glue is an easy way to get just a little sparkle.

Supplies: patterned paper (The Girls' Paperie); glitter glue (Ranger); acrylic snowflakes (Maya Road); decorative scissors (Fiskars); punch (EK Success); self-adhesive pearls, self-adhesive gems (The Paper Studio); doily (Wilton); rub-ons (Melissa Frances); other: Copic markers, baker's twine, vintage buttons

I had so much fun creating this placecard holder—I just pulled out different products and played with them to see what I could come up with. I started by altering the papier mâché egg, then went on the hunt for a base. I decided to turn a mini tart tin upside down because I loved its flared, scalloped look. I separated the egg and tin with a vintage milk bottle cap, but that left a gap I wanted to fill. I instantly thought of the *Tissue Paper Trim* from page 16, and this fringe worked perfectly; it helped support the egg and created a great Easter grass look. The only change I made to the technique was that I did not trim the edges with scallop scissors. Instead, I left the edges straight, which I thought helped reinforce the grass look I was going for.

Supplies: papier mâché egg (Michaels); paint (Making Memories); glitter glue, paint (Ranger); milk bottle cap, tart tin (Jenni Bowlin); flocked flowers (Vintage Street Market); crystal pin (Maya Road); ink (Clearsnap); other: chenille chick, Easter grass, seam binding, Copic marker

I wanted to add dimension to this festive, summery layout, so I decided to use the *Paper 3-D Embellishment* technique from page 106 on this layout. Instead of the pumpkins you see in the autumn chapter, I used stars to fit the theme of the layout. To make the stars, I punched four stars out of patterned paper, stacked them and stitched them together using a straight stitch on my sewing machine. Then I bent the edges upward to create the 3-D look. To give the stars a little twinkle, I accented the edges of each star layer using glitter glue. I continued the sparkly theme by accenting the edges of each patterned paper layer with glitter glue as well.

Supplies: patterned paper (Melissa Frances); chipboard (Maya Road, Jenni Bowlin); paint, blue ribbon embellishment (Jenni Bowlin); glitter glue (Ranger); alpha stickers (Making Memories, K&Company); decorative scissors (Fiskars); punch (EK Success); chipboard banner (Maya Road); rhinestones (Advantus); other: baker's twine, vintage crepe paper

This project brings the *Fabric Cabbage Roses* from page 56 out of spring and into summer. When I created the cabbage roses for this wedding card, I wanted them to have a unique texture. I decided using burlap and muslin would be a wonderful combination. I held the two strips together, but slightly offset, while twisting and wrapping, so both materials would show well in the finished flower. Have fun experimenting with different fabrics and textiles when making your cabbage roses. You can add lace, twine, ribbons and other items to the fabric strips to achieve different looks for your flowers.

Supplies: patterned paper (Pink Paislee); felt (CPE); embroidery floss (DMC); trim (Maya Road); self-adhesive pearl flowers (Jenni Bowlin); embossed sticker (K&Company); self-adhesive pearls (The Paper Studio); other: burlap, muslin, buttons, dictionary page

On this tag, I took the *Embellished Clear Button* technique from page 24 out of winter and transformed it with red, white and blue. What says summer more than Independence Day? After I gave these buttons a stars-and-stripes makeover, I formed them into a button bouquet. To do this, I threaded 24-gauge wire up through one buttonhole, down through the next, and then I twisted the wire ends together. After that, each button was accented with a self-adhesive pearl. Finally, I grouped all the buttons together, secured them with a piece of wire and tied a seam binding bow around the bunch to finish off the bouquet.

Supplies: patterned paper, rub-ons, self-adhesive pearls (Melissa Frances); wire (Darice); ink (Clearsnap); trim (Maya Road); clear buttons (Autumn Leaves); rhinestones (Advantus); gloss medium (Ranger); other: seam binding, baker's twine

I created the snowflakes you see on this tag using the steps from the *Altered Die Cut* from page 104. I applied two different shades of blue ink onto each snowflake, with the lighter ink at the center and the darker ink at the edges to create contrast. After inking the snowflakes, I accented each one using white ultra thick embossing enamel (UTEE). After the UTEE cooled, I applied glitter glue to add a little sparkle. The only change I made to the technique for this project was to add a rhinestone to the center of each snowflake for even more sparkle. A few simple changes give this technique from the autumn chapter a wonderful wintery feel.

Supplies: patterned paper (Vintage Street Market); tag, glitter glue, ink, ultra thick embossing enamel, embossing medium pen (Ranger); watercolor paper (C-Thru Ruler Company Art-C Collection); die (Sizzix); trim, acrylic snowflake (Maya Road); self-adhesive pearls (The Paper Studio); rhinestones (Doodlebug Design Inc., Queen & Co.); other: seam binding

Aunt Linda and Dad playing in a snow drift in the driveway of their childhood home.

Greenland, NH
Winter 1955

snow day

The *Altered Bottle Brush Tree* technique from page 90 can be used for any season! Creating this Independence Day star was fun and easy. I altered these trees by bleaching them, then I dyed the bottom end of the tree blue and the top red. I created the star shape by placing five trees together with their ends pointed outward and their stems meeting in the middle. If you would like to take this technique to yet another season, you can also arrange the trees into this same star shape to make a Christmas ornament. Just use smaller trees to make a smaller star. Dyeing the trees red or leaving them bleached and covering them in mica flakes would make gorgeous ornaments.

Supplies: tinsel garland, tissue garland (Bethany Lowe); chipboard, crystal star pins, ink spray (Maya Road); decorative scissors (Fiskars); self-adhesive pearls (The Paper Studio); glitter glue (Ranger); stickers (Making Memories); other: bottle brush trees, crepe paper, Copic marker, vintage sheet music, beads, baker's twine

I combined two techniques to alter the chipboard coffee pot on this card to make it look like a piece of vintage Flow Blue porcelain. First, I used paint, ink and ultra thick embossing enamel (UTEE) to alter the coffee pot following the steps for the *Embellished Chipboard Frame* on page 74. The process I followed was to emboss the chipboard piece with an embossing folder, then I painted the entire piece white. Once the white paint was dry, I accented the embossed areas using a navy blue acrylic paint. After the blue paint dried, I darkened the white areas with just a bit with creamy brown ink. Next, I embossed the blue areas using an embossing medium pen and clear UTEE. Once I was done with those steps, I used the technique from page 58 to decorate the edges of the coffee pot with platinum UTEE.

Supplies: patterned paper (Jenni Bowlin); clip art (Vintage Street Market); rub-ons (Melissa Frances); self-adhesive pearls (The Paper Studio); decorative scissors (Fiskars); chipboard coffee pot (Maya Road); paint, ultra thick embossing enamel, embossing medium pen, glitter glue (Ranger); embossing plate (Sizzix); ink (Clearsnap, Maya Road); embroidery floss (DMC); tiny attacher staples (Tim Holtz); other: vintage lace, baker's twine, vintage buttons

Erin go bragh!

May your bl[...] outn[...] t[...] shamrocks that grow.

3-17

There is no mistaking what occasion this card celebrates—all of the green gives it away! I started with shiny green shamrocks and thought they would look cute with pearl centers, but for more green, I colored each pearl using a green Copic marker. I also accented the back of the girl's dress with a bow created out of olive green seam binding. Since I did not have a spool of green thread to use in my sewing machine, I randomly stitched over the machine stitching as I did on the layout on pages 76–77 using green embroidery floss. If you want the theme of your project to be instantly recognizable, you can go overboard with color like I did here. Try pink and red for Valentine's Day and orange and black for Halloween!

Supplies: patterned paper (The Girls' Paperie); vintage trim, Dresden shamrocks, vintage milk bottle cap (Jenni Bowlin); self-adhesive pearls (The Paper Studio); embroidery floss (DMC); ink (Clearsnap); glitter glue (Ranger); tinted tape (Vintage Street Market); other: seam binding, Copic marker

My brother and I always loved waking up New Year's Day and running downstairs to see what neat party hats, horns and other noise makers our mom and dad would bring home from their New Year's Eve celebration. This memory inspired me to re-create the *Paper Party Hat* from page 82 to celebrate New Year's instead of a birthday. This scaled-down hat was created using a 4" × 5" (10cm × 13cm) piece of patterned paper. This card can be used as a greeting card to send to friends and family or as an invitation for a New Year's Eve party.

Supplies: patterned paper (Making Memories); ink (Clearsnap); decorative scissors (Fiskars); glitter glue (Ranger); self-adhesive pearls (The Paper Studio); clocks (Maya Road); other: crepe paper

happy New Year

At every graduation I've attended, including my own, the girls were always given a flower to carry. Because of this, I thought flowers would be the perfect accent for this layout. I created these felt roses using the *Paper Rose* technique on page 112. Instead of using a punch, I used a floral die and cut out the same flower three times. Then I created felt flowers just as I would have if I were working with paper. Because there are so many floral dies on the market right now, you can create a wide variety of flowers. Don't be afraid to experiment not only with different dies, but also different materials. You will be amazed at what you create!

Supplies: patterned paper, cabinet card (Jenni Bowlin); felt (CPE); pearls (The Paper Studio); doily (Wilton); punches (EK Success); die (Sizzix); ink (Clearsnap); other: felt leaves

I created this fairy ornament using a photo of my mom and two different techniques from previous chapters. I started this project with a family photo, as I did in the *Family Photo Embellishment* on page 66. I then combined this technique with the *Crepe Paper Doll* technique from page 84 to add a crepe paper dress to the photo as well as chenille stem arms and legs. To finish the project, I added lots of sparkle. I started with a rhinestone crown, then added chipboard wings that were coated with glitter glue and German glass glitter. The dress was given a thin coat of decoupage medium and sprinkled with glitter, then further embellished with glitter glue. Like the dolls on page 84, this ornament carries a bouquet of flocked flowers. These little touches bring this sparkling fairy to life.

Supplies: crepe paper (Designware); patterned paper (Anna Griffin Inc.); ink (Clearsnap); ink, chipboard wings (Maya Road); decorative scissors, punch (Fiskars); gloss medium, glitter glue (Ranger); vintage chenille stems, flocked flowers (Laura's Vintage Garden); other: seam binding, glitter

This is another project that combines two techniques you'll find in this book. The first I employed on this card can be found on page 94—the *Pearlescent Pigment Watercolors* technique. This technique added subtle, pretty colors to the card base. Next, I accented several silk flowers using the *Embellished Silk Flower* technique on page 44. For the flowers on this card, I only used one bold color instead of several pastel colors—this gives the flowers a more autumnal look. For extra sparkle, I adhered coarse crystal glitter to the flowers using glitter glue instead of decoupage medium.

Supplies: cabinet card (Jenni Bowlin); pearlescent pigment powder, pearlescent pigment spray, glitter glue (Ranger); rub-ons (Melissa Frances); felt (CPE); gold leafing pen (Krylon); glitter (EK Success); self-adhesive pearls (The Paper Studio); jewelry tag (American Tag Co.); other: Copic marker, silk flower, vintage button, baker's twine

"Believe in yourself, dream big and you will achieve," is the perfect sentiment for a graduation tag, and I thought a butterfly would be a good symbol for the tag as well. I used the *Paint and Ink Patina* technique from page 30 to embellish the chipboard butterfly I chose. Instead of using blue and brown for a patina effect, however, I painted the chipboard pieces with several different colors for a pastel rainbow look. Once the paint was dry, I covered each piece with gloss medium and glitter. To complete the look, I created the butterfly's body by attaching three self-adhesive pearls to the center. Changing the chipboard shape and the paint colors gives this technique a summery look.

Supplies: patterned paper (The Girls' Paperie); tag, pearlescent pigment powder, pearlescent pigment spray, glitter glue, gloss medium (Ranger); lace doily, punch (EK Success); ink (Clearsnap); embossing folder (Sizzix); rub-ons (Melissa Frances); chipboard butterfly, glitter (Maya Road); paint (Jenni Bowlin); self-adhesive pearls (The Paper Studio); other: vintage buttons, seam binding, vintage lace

Resources

The following companies manufacture products featured in this book. Please check your local retailers to find these materials, or go to a company's website for the latest product information. In addition, we have made every attempt to properly credit the items mentioned in this book. We apologize to any company that we have listed incorrectly, and we would appreciate hearing from you.

3ndypapir.no
www.3ndypapir.no

Adornit/Carolee's Creations
www.adornit.com

Advantus Corp.
www.advantus.com

American Tag Company
www.americantag.net

Anna Griffin
www.annagriffin.com

Art~C Mixed-Media Tools and Supplies
www.myartc.com

BasicGrey
www.basicgrey.com

Beacon Adhesives
www.beaconadhesives.com

Bethany Lowe Designs, Inc.
www.bethanylowe.com

Clearsnap
www.clearsnap.com

Clover
www.clover-usa.com

Cocoa Daisy
www.cocoadaisy.com

Copic Marker
www.copicmarker.com

Cosmo Cricket
www.cosmocricket.com

CPE
www.newimageco.biz

Crafty Secrets
www.craftysecrets.com

Creative Paperclay
www.paperclay.com

Creativity Inc.
www.creativityinc.com

Darice Inc.
www.darice.com

Déjà Views
www.dejaviews.com

Die Cuts With A View (DCWV)
www.diecutswithaview.com

The DMC Corporation
www.dmc-usa.com

Doodlebug Design Inc.
www.doodlebug.ws

EK Success Brands
www.eksuccess.com

Ellison
www.ellison.com

Fiskars
www.fiskars.com

German Corner LLC
www.germanplaza.com

The Girls' Paperie
www.thegirlspaperie.com

Graphic 45
www.g45papers.com

iLoveToCreate
www.ilovetocreate.com

Jenni Bowlin
www.jbsmercantile.com

K&Company
www.kandcompany.com

Krylon
www.krylon.com

Laura's Vintage Garden
www.etsy.com/shop/laurasvintagegarden

Lily Bee Design
www.lilybeedesign.com

Little Yellow Bicycle
www.mylyb.com

Making Memories
www.makingmemories.com

Mark Richards Enterprises, Inc.
www.markrichardsusa.com

Maya Road, LLC
www.mayaroad.net

Melissa Frances
www.melissafrances.com

My Mind's Eye
www.mymindseye.com

October Afternoon
www.octoberafternoon.com

The Paper Studio
www.paperstudio.com

Pebbles Inc.
www.pebblesinc.com

Pink Paislee
www.pinkpaislee.com

Plaid Enterprises, Inc.
www.plaidonline.com

Provo Craft
www.provocraft.com

Queen & Co.
www.queenandco.com

Ranger Industries, Inc.
www.rangerink.com

Sassafras Lass
www.sassafraslass.com

Sizzix
www.sizzix.com

Studio 490 by Wendy Vecchi
www.stampersanonymous.com

Tim Holtz idea-ology
www.timholtz.com/idea-ology

Vintage Street Market
www.vintagestreetmarket.com

Wilton Industries
www.wilton.com

Zucker Feather Products
www.zuckerfeather.com

Index

Dedication

This book is dedicated to my mom and dad for always making each holiday, birthday and special occasion extra special. It's because of you two that I have a love for the seasons and all that they bring. I have many wonderful childhood memories from each season, but I must admit the summer Richard and I made our homemade Slip 'n Slide and completely destroyed the front yard is one of my favorites. Gosh, did we ever have fun. I'm glad this is now in the past and time has allowed the humor to be seen.

Always know I love you both so much.

Acknowledgments

I want to thank everyone at F+W Media, Inc. and North Light Books for putting so much of their time and energy into creating this book. I know this never would have come to be without all of your behind-the-scenes work and dedication. Thank you.

Thank you to these four very special friends. You all are a wonderful group for support and I cannot imagine going through this process without you:

· Caroline, your continued friendship and support is something I will always cherish. You have taught me so much about this industry, but the most important lesson you have taught me is to believe in myself.

· Lisa, you survived yet another book with me and our friendship is still going strong.

· Ronda, who would have known when we met and roomed together in Mykonos, Greece, that such a wonderful friendship would develop. I feel so blessed to call you my friend.

· Wendy, once again I have been blessed with all your encouraging e-mails, always positive and always supportive. You are the best!

I thank all of you for your patience, support and encouragement, but most of all your friendship.

Big thanks to Christine Doyle for believing in me enough to create a second book.

Thank you to my editors, Jennifer Claydon and Kristy Conlin. It has been a true delight working with you. Your guidance throughout this process has been most appreciated. You two are the best!

Thank you to photographer Christine Polomsky. It was a pleasure getting to work with you once again. You are always so sweet and patient in your studio.

Special thanks to iLoveToCreate, a Duncan Enterprises Company, for generously donating the adhesives I used on projects in this book.

Thank you to all the wonderful companies who so generously donated their products: Cocoa Daisy; Fiskars; German Corner, LLC; Crafty Secrets Heartwarming Vintage; iLoveTo-Create, a Duncan Enterprises Company; Jenni Bowlin; Laura's Vintage Garden; Little Yellow Bicycle; Maya Road; Pink Paislee; Ranger Ink; Sassafras Lass; Stampers Anonymous; Studio 490 by Wendy Vecchi; The Girls' Paperie; Tim Holtz idea-ology; Vintage Street Market; Art-C Mixed Media; and 3ndypapir.no.

About the Author

Lisa M. Pace loves all things that sparkle, show dimension and look vintage. Her first memory of creating a project was as a three-year-old child, sitting at the kitchen table with her mom. From then on, she devoted her life to honing her skills as a mixed-media artist. Her most recent artistic outlet has been papercrafting. Since 2005, she has had numerous items published in magazines and idea books. In May 2007, Lisa was selected as one of five master scrapbookers in Martha Stewart's scrapbooking contest, and she was chosen as a 2008 *Memory Makers* Master. In 2010, Lisa's highly popular technique-based book *Delight in the Details* was published.

Lisa's work is marked by her ability to rethink and reuse. Her commitment to always add that special embellishment sets her work apart from others. Lisa currently lives in Frisco, Texas, with her husband and two daughters. She says that the heart of her designs is "in the details."

To learn more about Lisa, visit her at www.lisapace.com.

Delight in the Seasons. Copyright © 2012 by Lisa M. Pace. Manufactured in China. All rights reserved. The patterns and drawings in this book are for the personal use of the reader. By permission of the author and publisher, they may be either hand-traced or photocopied to make single copies, but under no circumstances may they be resold or republished. It is permissible for the purchaser to create the designs contained herein and sell them at fairs, bazaars and craft shows. No other part of this book may be reproduced in any form or by any electronic or mechanical means including information storage and retrieval systems without permission in writing from the publisher, except by a reviewer who may quote brief passages in a review. Published by North Light Books, an imprint of F+W Media, Inc., 10150 Carver Road, Cincinnati, Ohio 45242. (800) 289-0963. First Edition.

16   15   14   13   12   5   4   3   2   1

DISTRIBUTED IN CANADA BY FRASER DIRECT
100 Armstrong Avenue
Georgetown, ON, Canada L7G 5S4
Tel: (905) 877-4411

DISTRIBUTED IN THE U.K. AND EUROPE BY
F&W MEDIA INTERNATIONAL
Brunel House, Newton Abbot, Devon, TQ12 4PU, England
Tel: (+44) 1626 323200, Fax: (+44) 1626 323319
Email: enquiries@fwmedia.com

DISTRIBUTED IN AUSTRALIA BY CAPRICORN LINK
P.O. Box 704, S. Windsor NSW, 2756 Australia
Tel: (02) 4577-3555

SRN: W0940
ISBN-13: 978-1-4403-1363-9

www.fwmedia.com

EDITORS Jennifer Claydon & Kristy Conlin

DESIGNER Geoff Raker

PRODUCTION COORDINATOR Greg Nock

PHOTOGRAPHY Christine Polomsky

Metric Conversion Chart

To convert	to	multiply by
Inches	Centimeters	2.54
Centimeters	Inches	0.4
Feet	Centimeters	30.5
Centimeters	Feet	0.03
Yards	Meters	0.9
Meters	Yards	1.1

Looking for more inspiration?

Make your holidays and celebrations even more memorable—visit CreateMixedMedia.com for delightful **FREE BONUS TECHNIQUES** from Lisa Pace!

You'll learn step by step how to create two beautiful embellishments out of the humblest of materials—crepe paper and felt. These embellishments will add the perfect detail to cards, layouts, décor and more.

Crepe Paper Flowers
www.createmixedmedia.com/delight-crepe-flowers

Felt Roses
www.createmixedmedia.com/delight-felt-roses

And join the fun at

 www.facebook.com/CreateMixedMedia.com

 @cMixedMedia

A Great Community to Inspire You Every Day!

create mixed media

Inventive free projects, tutorials and e-books, blogs, podcasts, reviews, special offers and more!

CreateMixedMedia.com and ShopMixedMedia.com

For inspiration delivered to your inbox, sign up for our free e-mail newsletter.

NORTH LIGHT BOOKS

Check out these great North Light Craft titles

Creative Foundations
40 Scrapbook and Mixed-Media Techniques to Build Your Artistic Toolbox.

Delight in the Details
40+ Techniques for Charming Embellishments and Accents.

These and other fine North Light Craft titles are available at your local craft retailer, bookstore or online supplier, or visit ShopMixedMedia.com.